PRAISE FOR HEROES OF THE STAGE

"What a great read for anyone who wants to better understand the bond between our Service-members and Country Music Artists – they are often one in the same. As a recently retired Army Combat Veteran, trust me when I say that music truly does bring a little taste of home when you're deployed to the badlands! HOOAH Travis!"

– Rick Brown
U.S. Army 1st SG (Retired)
Founder/President, Rick Brown Communications, LLC

Entertaining. Educational. Inspiring. "Heroes of the Stage" is all this and more! Marine Veteran Travis McVey is a visionary entrepreneur who has combined his love of country music and passion for serving fellow veterans into an imminently readable and immensely enjoyable book about country music stars – past and present – who served our country before taking the stage. This book is a "must have" for all country music fans and veterans!

– Phil Dyer, CFP, RLP, CPCC
West Point Graduate and America's Entrepreneur Strategist

"Two subjects neat and dear to my heart, country music and the men and women of our armed forces. As an Army Brat growing up on military bases all over the world I learned first-hand of the sacrifices our military and their families make for us every day. "Heroes of the Stage" is a heart-warming read that highlights and honors some of country music's greats that have served our country with dedication and also inspired us with their music."

– Kate of *"Lucy Angel"*

HEROES OF THE STAGE

HEROES OF THE STAGE

➤ COUNTRY SERVING COUNTRY ◀

BY TRAVIS L. McVEY

HEROES OF THE STAGE:
Copyright © 2011 by Travis L. McVey

ISBN: 978-0-615-45434-4

LCCN: 2011930282

CIP data on file with the Library of Congress

Published in the United States by
Hero Spirit Publishing
312 Lind Street
McMinnville, TN 37110

Cover Art: Tarrier Design

Cover Concept Design: Double Diamond
501 Union Street, Suite 201
Nashville, TN 37219
Manufactured in the United States of America

Photos courtesy of Photofest unless otherwise noted.

Artist illustraions by Nina Didenko

Book design by Sue Balcer of JustYourType.biz

Books are available in quantity for promotional or premium use. Write to Director of Special Sales, Hero Spirit Publishing, 312 Lind Street, McMinnville, TN 37110, for information on discounts and terms or call (615) 483-5155. www.heroesofthestage.com

For Logan John, my wonderful son

❖ CONTENTS ❖

PART ONE
U.S. MARINES 5

*"When I think about Country Music,
I think about America."*

Johnny Cash (U.S. Air Force)

✦ ACKNOWLEDGMENTS ✦

This book is the result of many influences in my life and as well as many inspirational people who have encouraged me to take action and tell this story. My mom and dad, who always told me to work hard and to pursue my dreams. To my big brother (Brent Tooter McVey) and his friends, who always used to beat me up when I was young and wanted to tag along or play ball with them - you gave me drive and made me stronger. To the United States Marine Corps, for teaching me what Honor, Courage and Commitment really mean. To Bud Klika at the SBDC, for pushing me to live my dream of owning my own business. To Will Cheek at BONE MCALLASTER and NORTON, for telling me to call Robert Lipman about HEROES VODKA. To Paul Kruse, for telling me everything is going to be ok with my Trademarks and his hard work to see it through. To Robert Lipman, for believing in me and sharing my vision of wanting to develop a brand that would help Veterans. To Angela, Scot, Jennifer and Jackie at Double Diamond Design, for hearing all of my ideas and making them a reality. To Jason McMurray, for being my friend and giving me good solid advice time and time again. To everyone at NaVOBA and BUY VETERAN, for letting me know that I'm not alone and that there are over 3 million Veteran Business Owners out there like myself. To Larry Broughton and Phil Dyer and all the Victory Success System inaugural class, for encouraging me to write this book and giving me the tools to do so and for your passion for helping aspiring Veteran business owners. To all of the artists, who shared their stories with me and giving me the honor to write them down to share with everyone. I thank you for your service and for your wonderful music and the way you bring people together. To my son Logan, for just inspiring me every day to be the best that I can be and the way he makes me so proud to be his Dad. To all my friends at the Grown Man Frat House (GMFH), you know who you are…To all of my friends, especially Jason and Jo, and to my family, for your encouraging words and continued support. To my two brother Marines Richard and Tommy, who gave the ultimate sacrifice for our Nation - you touched my life in so many ways and I miss you guys so very much. I can still see us driving home on leave together in Tommy's old truck, listening to Country music and smiling and laughing on the trips home. Last, but certainly not least, to all of the HEROES on and off the stage who have served this nation in uniform, you continue to inspire all of us and keep us free, we salute you…

"If you can hold your listener, hold their attention, and you're sure you know what you're doing and know that you're communicating. You've got a song you're singing from your gut, you want that audience to feel it in their gut."

Johnny Cash (U.S. Air Force)

❧ INTRODUCTION ❧

There is something about Country Music that captures the heart and soul of America. There is also something else that seems to go hand in hand with Country Music and that is a love for our Country and for the men and women who serve in the military. This book only covers those artists who are living today, but certainly recognizes those artists who have been called home to their Creator and will be honored in the TAPS section of this book. If, for some reason, I overlooked an artist I do apologize and I certainly appreciate their service and their contribution to Country music.

Over the years, there has, it seems, a slew of patriotic or military typed songs performed by Country Artists. It may surprise you to find out though, of all the Country Artists, the ones <u>WHO</u> actually served and wore this nation's uniform. I know I was when I first was inspired to write this book. It truly was an inspirational and rewarding journey though as I did my research for this book and found out who they were. I hope you, the reader, feels the same way after reading HEROES OF THE STAGE. Some of them you will already have known about and some may come as a complete surprise to you. Some are more famous and well known than others, but all of them served this Nation for all of us and deserve our sincere thanks as well as our respect. As you come acquainted with these Artists who served, you might just become a new fan or a fan all over again.

The inspiration came for this book after I met and became close friends with Country Artist and fellow Marine Stephen Cochran in 2010 at the Country Radio Seminar (CRS) in Nashville, TN. After hearing Stephen's story and listening to his music, I instantly became a fan. I also noticed in a lot of our conversations Stephen would say, "such and such Country Artist was a Marine or he was in the Army." I was like, "WOW, that is so cool, I didn't know that." I also knew that many didn't know that and like myself, would really think that was pretty awesome. It also came to me that, "You know what? People need to know this and people want to know this and especially our younger generation needs to know this. Most importantly though, other Veterans need to know this." Why? some people may ask. Because serving your Country means something to most Americans and it is a great example to so many. Only about 2% of Americans ever serve in the military, so it is actually a close knit community of people who have shared some very special moments and memories. It inspires us to see that these Artists served their Country in uniform and helped protect our freedoms. So when they sing about America or the military or war, whether it be for or against, it takes on a new meaning because it is firsthand knowledge and it truly comes from the heart and soul. I've seen it first hand when one of the Artists performed a particular song about war at a VFW in Nashville. This song about war resonated and touched everyone in that room from the WW 2 Veteran to the Korean Veteran, to the Vietnam Veteran, to the Gulf War Veteran and to the Iraq and Afghan Veterans. It brought them all together for that moment in time. It made them feel young again, it made them feel truly alive again, it made them strong again, it made them see their buddies again, it made their chest swell with pride again, it made some of them cry and let loose some pain they really needed to let go of. Most importantly, it brought all of us together feeling a sense of pride and gratitude for our Country and for the men and women who serve in the military. After the performance was over, everyone seemed to open up more and share their stories from the service or problems they were having today dealing with something that happened to them. Some say music can soothe the soul and in the hands of a Veteran who happens to be a Country Music Artist, I saw how powerful it can be that day, of not only soothing the wounded souls of our warriors, but opening that soul up so it can begin to heal.

There were also people that day who hadn't served in the military, but you should have seen their faces as well, listening to us talk about our service and our stories and experiences. They were totally enthralled seeing us open up and talking so openly and enthusiastically with each other. Even though they didn't understand some of our acronyms or sayings, they loved it just the same. So my hope is this book will do the same by bringing us together, if only for awhile and open us up in understanding one another and the value of what serving one's Country really means for Country Artists who have served…Maybe and just maybe one day soon the Country Music Hall of Fame will have a special exhibit for all the HEROES OF THE STAGE, showcasing those Artists and their pictures and uniforms and other memorabilia from their time in the service…

PART ONE
THE MARINES

George Jones

Ray Price

Stephen Cochran

Jerry Foster

Jamey Johnson

Josh Gracin

Jason Michael Carroll

*"My heroes are the ones who survived
doing it wrong, who made mistakes,
but recovered from them."*

Bono

GEORGE JONES

(United States Marine)

GEORGE GLENN JONES, also known as the "Possum", got his start in the country music business many decades ago. He was born September 12, 1931 in Saratoga, Texas. Jones started singing as a kid at seven years old after his parents bought him his radio and he heard some country music songs. He got his own guitar and played on the streets of his hometown in Texas for tips. He graduated from the streets to playing cover tunes in some of the local radio stations. He moved on to Honky Tonks in the region and sang many of the popular tunes in the day, including songs by Hank Williams and Roy Acuff. Once he married Tammy Wynette, one of the earliest and most famous female country singers of the business, his career took off and then nose-dived before he salvaged it for a second time.

While Jones is known for his music, he is less known for the time he spent in the military. Jones signed up for the United States Marine Corps in 1950. His unit was trained in California and that is where he remained during his service career, even though the Korean War was going on. George did not serve overseas before his term was up in November of 1953. He was honorably discharged and went back to his music roots.

Unfortunately, Jones became known for his wild lifestyle once he exited the military. He was a very heavy drinker and admitted to starting the day out with a mixed drink. One story that is prevalent when talking about George Jones is when he rode a lawnmower in to town to buy alcohol. His first wife, named Dorothy, was determined to keep him from the alcohol one night. She did so by hiding all of the keys to the vehicles in their garage and left him home alone. She did not, however, remove the lawnmower keys. Jones has said it was only an eight mile trip in to town, so he jumped on it and away he went – even though it took an hour and a half to get there.

Jones was divorced from Dorothy within a year and then he married Shirley, his second wife. He focused on his music career and after recording various songs under alias names, he experimented with his sound. He signed with Starday Records in 1954. His first album was called "No Money In This Deal" and he got his first top five hit from it, with "Why Baby Why".

Under the name of Thumper Jones, he recorded an album for Mercury Records in 1958. The song called "White Lightning" was Jones' first number one hit in 1959 from that album. Other hits from it included Jones second #1 hit called "Tender Years" in 1961.

Jones began writing his own songs after that and

switched between the labels of Musicor, Mercury and United Artists. He also sang a few duets during the mid-60s with Melba Montgomery, Gene Pitney and Brenda Carter. He had a few other top ten songs, and had a relatively uneventful decade until Jones divorced Shirley in 1968, after having two sons together.

In 1969, he met and married Tammy Wynette. Jones joined forces at Wynette's Epic record label and started getting lots more attention for his singing. Their tumultuous marriage produced some awesome duets, such as "Near You", "Golden Ring" and "We're Gonna Hold On". They also had a daughter together. Georgette Jones is the only child of two members of the Country Music Hall of Fame and many consider that Country Music Royalty. She is a very talented singer and entertainer herself. Georgette and her father wrote and performed a song together that is very moving titled, "You And Me And Time." Georgette also has a book coming out in July 2011 titled, "The Three Of Us: Growing Up With Tammy And George."

George and Tammy were wildly popular on stage, but behind closed doors it was another story. His alcoholism had grown to be a large problem, but then there were other problems with cocaine addiction, tax errors, bad management and debt he and Tammy had. Jones and Wynette also had an incident where she woke up one night to find him gone. She drove to a local bar and spotted a lawnmower parked out front. Once she walked in, Jones said to his drinking buddies, "I knew she'd find me." Wynette and

Jones divorced in 1975, after many arguments and widely publicized domestic fights.

Jones' addiction to cocaine and alcohol became so bad, it overtook his life. He quickly earned the nickname No Show Jones. Due to his unreliability for being at a show – either he was too drunk or high to perform – many promoters ended up canceling their shows, making his money woes even worse. In 1979, he was recorded as having missed or canceling 50 shows in just one year.

Jones' alcoholism got worse and he ended up in the hospital in a mental ward. Jones continued on singing and performing once he was released. He wrote a few songs and ended up with his biggest hit when he was between wives. "He Stopped Loving Her Today" was a #1 hit in 1980 and won many awards. It received a Grammy, an ACM, A CMA and a Music City News award - every category it was nominated in that year it won for. His last #1 hit was in 1983 with "I Always Get Lucky With You".

George met his fourth wife Nancy in 1981 and married her in 1983. She became his manager and directed him away from the poor influences of his life. In 1984, she told him he was going to die if he didn't clean up his act. Over the course of the next year, he was in and out of rehab seven times while he tried to sober up. They have had a strong marriage and Nancy has helped Jones to get sober and stay that way for years. She has helped him regain a strong and positive reputation in the music industry.

Jones has had over 150 hits through his six decades of

singing in the country genre. His awards include 3 Grammys, six CMAs, three ACMs and three Music City News awards. He has also been very popular as a duet partner for modern country artists. He has recorded or appeared in videos with Garth Brooks, Randy Travis, Vince Gill, Shelby Lynne, Sammy Kershaw, Patty Loveless, Brad Paisley, Alan Jackson and James Taylor. Music videos for Hank Williams and Vince Gill both include spots where Jones is famously riding a lawn tractor on the side of the road, in reference to his arguments with former wives'. In the late 1990s, George recorded a few songs that were hits, but not chart toppers. They were called "High Tech Redneck" And "I Don't Need Your Rocking Chair".

Jones was inducted in to the Country Music Hall of Fame in 1992. He is classified as a Living Legend because even though he is still alive and making music, it isn't played on the popular airwaves as the sound of country music has evolved over the years. In 1996, he released an autobiography titled, "I Lived to Tell It All." Jones worked on the book for years, but finally decided to get it published when he kept hearing lie after lie being told about his life. He wanted to clear the air on incidents that were reported in the press and set the record straight. The book was popular and climbed to the #6 spot on the New York Times Bestseller List.

In 1999, he had another relapse which resulted in a bad car accident where he almost lost his life. There was an open bottle of alcohol in the truck he was driving and police discovered it in their investigation. Jones was cited, given a fine and forced into rehab once again. He has stayed out of the limelight with such behavior and appears to have stayed sober since then.

Jones hit the charts in the 2000s again as a duet partner. He was in on making Garth Brooks' song, "Beer Run" and on Shooter Jennings' "4th of July" song. The songs didn't make it in the top ten, but they kept Jones on the charts long enough to make him have hit records in every decade since the 1950s. Not many artists can make that same claim. Also in 2002, Mr. Jones received the National Medal of Arts Honor from the 43rd President of the United States George W. Bush, a fellow Texan. The medal is our nation's highest honor for achievements in the arts world.

Jones is still singing, but his shows are in smaller arenas and not as frequently. He performs close to 100 times a year with a smaller song set as well. Even though music was his first business, Jones and his manager wife have built a brand around a few products. Jones has created a line of breakfast sausages named after him which he promotes. He also released a product called White Lightening, which was a type of bottled water.

Even with all of the awards and accomplishments that George Jones has received there is but one title that separates him from so many and makes him one of the Heroes of the Stage and that is the title he earned in becoming a United States Marine. George is very proud of his service in the Marines and is very supportive of our men and women in the military. Mr. Jones is truly one of the legends when it comes to the Heroes Of The Stage...

Tammy Wynette and George Jones (circa 1970s)

Hee Haw (TV series 1969-93) (CBS-TV: 1969-71,
Gaylord Prods. syndication: 1971-93)
Shown c. 1985, from left: guest George Jones, host Roy Clark

HERO OF THE STAGE

George Jones (USMC)

"The story of the Veterans should be told. That's our history. It was a global event that is worthy of our respect."

George Jones (USMC)

RAY PRICE

(United States Marine)

RAY PRICE was born January 12, 1926 in Perryville, Texas. As a child, he learned how to sing and play the guitar at his mom's home in Dallas and his dad's ranch. After he graduated from high school, he briefly tried college. He then signed up with the United States Marine Corp in 1944 and earned his eagle, globe and anchor, and served until 1946. Once he was honorably discharged from the Marine Corps, he went to college to become a veterinarian. At night, instead of studying for classes he started to perform in local honky tonks. It was by chance that he stumbled on to a career in country music. Price earned early on the nickname of Cherokee Cowboy.

In 1948, Price began singing country music on a radio station and was asked to join Big D Jamboree the next year after they heard him sing. An executive with Columbia Records heard him singing and offered him a contract in 1951. Price and the band split ways as he went to Nashville to pursue a career and they didn't.

Once Price made it to Nashville, he was roommates

with Hank Williams for a short time before his death. Hank Williams offered to show Price the ropes and allowed him to open a few shows for him. Williams heavily influence Price's early works and even helped record some of the music for it. Once he died, Price led his band for a couple years until they disbanded. Price performed on the Grand Ole Opry several times in his early career. Due to his friend's death, Price didn't perform or release any new music until 1954. After a few songs, he faded in to the background and wrote songs and had an idea. He started a band with several other startups in Nashville at the time. The other members included Johnny Paycheck, Willie Nelson, Johnny Bush and Roger Miller. They played and recorded music together until the mid-1960s. As they became famous in their own right, members left and new ones came in to make their marks on the industry.

His first #1 song was a honky tonk tune called "Crazy Arms" and it hit the top of the charts in 1956 and stayed there for 20 weeks – five months! It was also named the song of the year for the same year. This song's success is what started his career. After that, he followed it up with 23 songs that hit the Top 10. Some of those songs included "My Shoes Keep Walking Back to You" and "I've Got a New Heartache".

Price continued to sing honky tonk songs, but also branched out to include an orchestra in his hit song "Danny Boy" in 1967. The staunch honky tonk fans did not like his new sound, but fans who liked classical music sounds sure did. Some of his songs also held appeal in the pop genre, so Price had a wide range of audiences to play for.

During the 1970s, Price had only a few releases and a couple of songs that turned in to hits. He also switched record labels many times throughout the 1970s and the 1980s. He had even fewer songs released in the 1980s.

During his long career, Price won two ACM Awards, two Grammy Awards and a CMA Award. Price entered the Country Music Hall of Fame in 1996.

Price recorded an album in 2002 titled Time. In 2007, Price recorded an album which had musical accompaniment from Willie Nelson and Merle Haggard. The three briefly toured together to promote the album. He continues to make music and perform in venues across the United States. His genre of music is more on the Gospel side now instead of country music songs. Price performs regular shows on the stage in Branson, Missouri. Mr. Price has served his country as a United States Marine and as a legendary Country Music Artist and is one of the Heroes of the Stage...

HERO OF THE STAGE

Ray Price (USMC)

"There are only two kinds of people that understand Marines: Marines and the enemy. Everyone else has a second-hand opinion."

Gen. William Thornson, U.S. Army

STEPHEN COCHRAN

(Stephen Cochran Collection)

(United States Marine)

STEPHEN COCHRAN was born September 17, 1979 in Pikeville, Kentucky, but was basically raised in Nashville's songwriting community. He watched his Dad, Steve Cochran, wrestle with the machinery of Music Row as a struggling songwriter and artist. Country greats Bobby Bare and the late Del Reeves are just a few of the characters that influenced Cochran's early music home life. When Stephen was also 4 years old he began spending summers with his grandparents in Waterford, Michigan. Some of his closest friends are from that time in his life and he considers Michigan just as much a hometown as Kentucky and Tennessee. Cochran cultivated an interest in music beginning at Hunters Lane Comprehensive High School in Nashville, Tennessee. Later he honed his musical craft in his college days at Western Kentucky University with a development deal with Epic Records. He worked his self through college writing and playing guitar. While he was at Western, he also played rugby and lacrosse and had been recently named the Captain of the Lacrosse team. Then as everyone remembers our world forever changed on September 11th, 2001. Stephen was just a young college junior but was transfixed, along with the rest of our nation, when he learned of the terrorist attacks on the Twin Towers in New York and in Washington, D.C. at the Pentagon. Stephen being the man he is decided that very same day that he was going to enlist in the military to defend our nation. "It wasn't even a decision, it was just "gotta do it," Cochran told me. A country like ours that allows us to live our dreams as a job, any time that they need you to stand up and protect it was just driven into me. Patriotism is just in my family." The very next day, Stephen went and enlisted in the United States Marine Corps. "I didn't tell my parents or my fiancé at the time," Cochran said. "I just did it." Cochran was very driven and determined to get into the fight. He looked at some recruiting material at the recruiter's office and saw a film of the elite Marine Recon and said, "that is what I want to do!" The recruiter told him he would have to enlist as an 03, which is the infantry and then have to qualify to be in Marine Recon. Well, once this determined young hard charger set his mind to something it didn't take him long to qualify and volunteer to serve in the elite Marine Light Armored Reconnaissance 1st Marine Expeditionary Force. He and his unit then headed straight to Iraq. Immediately following his tour in Iraq, they were deployed to Afghanistan and while on combat patrol Sergeant Cochran was injured in combat, leaving his back broken in 6 pieces and his legs paralyzed. This young man was then told he would never walk again and was sent home to America. Finally, with Stephen's determination, coupled with a successful experimental medical treatment by the doctors at the VA Medical Center known as kyphoplasty and an extensive rehabilitation, he was able to walk again and return to an active lifestyle.

He then teamed up with other Country music artists and began performing with a big supporter of Veterans himself, John Rich and the MuzikMafia around Nashville. He wrote songs with his good friend from the band Trailer Choir Vinny Hickerson and eventually started their own writer's group. In 2007, he began Armed Forces Entertainment tours of the Middle East, and scores of benefit appearances on behalf of his fellow veterans. Stephen has a deep love for his country and for the men and women who have served in the military. It comes from a family background of service. His grandfather was in the Air Force for 26 years and his other grandpa retired from the Army. Stephen once told me, "You know, when you're a songwriter or a singer, or an artist in country music, you realize that this is the only country where you can take a dream and make it a business and turn it into a reality."

In 2009, the VA asked Stephen to be the face of their research and development. Cochran also wrote their new theme song, titled "Hope" and the VA is using it in their national campaign to help Veterans. Stephen said when interviewed by the Nashville local News Channel 5 WTVF, 11th February 2010, "I'm one of the only combat vets from this era in country music, and I need to use that platform to help things change and give hope back."

I first met Stephen at the Country Music Seminar (CRS) in 2010 by my long time friend and fellow Marine Lee McKennon, who is a business partner of Stephen's and the General Manager of Rock Solid Security located here in Nashville, Tennessee as well. Lee had been telling me a little bit about him but it just didn't register. He kept saying I have a friend who is also a Marine Veteran who is doing some work for the VA and he would like to meet you. I had just founded my own business Hero Spirit LLC, dba HEROES Vodka and Lee knew I was looking for someone to help out with that. For some reason, I had this vision pop in my head of this old crusty Marine who worked for the VA and I was looking for someone who could relate to this new generation of veterans and who could play music as well. Well I certainly was surprised when I met Stephen and we hit it off instantly. Since then we became very close friends, I'm proud to say. When you just spend a few moments with Stephen, his personality is infectious and you can see he really means it when he wants to help veterans and give back what he can to those brave men and women who serve and have served our nation. I also told him I was the Regional Rep for the National Veteran Owned Business Association (NaVOBA) and their BUY VETERAN campaign. So when they were looking themselves for someone in country music to be their National Spokesperson, I told them I have the perfect guy. Now Stephen spends a lot of his time promoting Veteran owned businesses and educating the public to buy from a Veteran owned business and recruiting other veterans to join up at www.buyveteran.com and list their businesses on that registry so the public can easily identify and find them when they need a particular product or service. In October of 2010, Stephen was asked by the Commandant of the Marine Corps to do an event for the Semper Fi Fund at Marine Barracks in D.C. and this organization is also very close to Stephen's heart. (For more information on the Semper Fi Fund and how you can help, go to www.semperfifund. org). Also, during that same trip Mark Woods, the founder of Operation Troop Aid (OTA) (www.operationtroopaid.org) another organization that Stephen loves to support, asked Stephen since he was going to be in the area could he do and event for shipping care packages over to the troops in Baltimore at the Baltimore Raven's stadium. "Of course," he said, "I would love to!" So he invited me along and I set up an interview for him with NaVOBA's Vetrepreneur magazine in their Nov/Dec issue. This was during the time they were also interviewing him not only for the magazine but to be their National Spokesperson. Matthew Pavelek, the Director of Communications for NaVOBA, conducted the interview and asked Stephen a series of questions. Stephen said during the interview, "What's more American than buying from veterans? Veterans are hard-working, loyal and dependable so you're going to get high-quality products or services. It's really a win-win for everybody." He also went on to say, "Standing up and saying you're a veteran and being part of NaVOBA and the BUY VETERAN movement and listing your business in the directory so people can find your business is one of the greatest tools I can think of having." As the voice of the Buy Veteran campaign, Cochran lends his talents and star power to promote the advantageous impacts of Americans purchasing products and services from veteran-owned businesses. His inspirational and triumphant story of bravery conquering adversity echoes the bold entrepreneurial spirit shared by all of America's 3 million veteran-owned businesses.

In a town where an artist's "story" is routinely embellished by teams of publicists, Cochran's background is as refreshingly real as his music. His debut album captured critical raves and earned three stars in Country Weekly. The first album also had three songs that made the Billboard Top 40. In the introduction of this book I talked about an artist who performed at a VFW in Nashville and how that song resonated and touched everyone in that room that day and brought us together; veterans and non-veterans alike. That artist was Stephen Cochran and that is a day I will never forget. I asked Stephen if he would come down to my VFW post 1291 and perform that day and in his usual manner he said, "I would love to!" He performed one of his songs that is very special and personal to him titled, "When A Hero Falls". It is a song he wrote after losing a very close friend in the war in Afghanistan and he wrote it from the heart and performs it from the heart.

It's often said that great country music is built on a foundation of real-life stories and soul-deep family tradition. He has told me numerous times if you date a song writer or a friend or family member of one; you're more than likely going to end up in a song. I have seen that first hand and boy can he write. I won't reveal the one he wrote about me but I made him change the names to protect the innocent. (lol) I'll just give you a little hint, "GMFH" and I'm sure it will be a big hit. Semper Fi brother! Stephen Cochran is definitely a life-size superstar next door, a combat veteran with a penchant for delivering when the curtain goes up. His song's mel familiar, country genres into appealing current blends. His love of country and passionate support of the courageous men and women who serve and have served in America's military make him one of the Heroes of the Stage...

Jon and I before a raid north of Kandahar, as part of Special Operations with 22nd M.E.U first push on Taliban. 4 months before my injury. *(Stephen Cochran Collection)*

Gen. James T. Conway 34th Commandant of the Marine Corps and Stephen Cochran. *(Stephen Cochran Collection)*

Stephen Cochran presenting the 35th Commandant of the Marine Corps General Amos with a gift from Tennessee. *(Travis McVey Collection)*

L-R: Travis McVey (Author, Heroes Vodka Founder, USMC) Lee McKennon (Rock Solid Security, USMC), Mark Woods (OTA Founder, USN), Stephen Cochran (Singer/Songwriter, USMC), Bart Butler (Rock Solid Security) and Mark Erhardt (Musician, USA) taken for an Operation Troop Aid event. *(Travis McVey Collection)*

HERO OF THE STAGE

(Photo by: Cpl. Samuel A. Nasso)

Stephen Cochran (USMC)

*"A Marine is a Marine. I set that policy two weeks ago –
there's no such thing as a former Marine.
You're a Marine, just in a different uniform and
you're in a different phase of your life. But you'll
always be a Marine because you went to Parris Island,
San Diego or the hills of Quantico.
There's no such thing as a former Marine."*

**General James F. Amos,
35th Commandant of the Marine Corps**

JERRY FOSTER

(Jerry Foster Collection)

(United States Marine)

JERRY GALEN FOSTER was born November 19, 1935 in a log house in Tallapoosa, MO whose population was 59 people. He was raised on music and hard work and from the age of 9, he travelled beside his father and their team of mules, raising cotton and corn. While at school, he earned extra money and by money I mean cents, in what Jerry would say by selling poems to his school seniors. His father bought him a guitar at the age of 5 and taught him to play a few chords and soon Jerry was taking part in the family get-togethers. Jerry graduated high school from Gideon High in MO in 1953. A natural performer, he eventually hit the road and earned money as a picker. Then he enlisted in the United States Marine Corps and earned his eagle, globe and anchor in Paris Island, South Carolina. Jerry attained the rank of Sergeant while he was in the Marine Corps and the Corps holds a very special place in his heart still today. My mom and Jerry have become very close friends over the years and I have had the pleasure to meet Jerry on a few occasions and he is always such a delight to talk to. I remember the first night Stephen Cochran and I met him at the Commadore in Nashville where he puts on a spectacular writer and performer's night once a month. Truly a must see if you're ever in the Nashville area. There is always a special bond between Marines and it was evident that night when us three got together and shared some stories from when we were in the Marines. Whenever you do a search on Jerry over the internet, in his bio it always states not only a farmer and singer songwriter, but a Marine as well. As the saying goes, "Once A Marine, Always Marine." Jerry still has that fire in his step and loves to perform and always has that signature grin that makes everyone want to smile and have a good time.

While in the Marines, he also formed a local group and played weekends when he could. He began playing melodies to his poems and this led to a recording deal in 1958, with the Houston-based Backbeat label. Foster's popularity began to grow, and he secured his first TV series on WSAF Savannah, Georgia. He then moved to KFVS-TV in Cape Girardeau, Missouri, with his own show and also as talent booker. He is also known by many as Foster and Rice for the many hits they co-wrote together. It was at a show in Poplar Bluff, Missouri, that he met Bill Rice. They found themselves trading song ideas and soon guitarist Roland Jones entered the picture. He suggested that Jerry and Bill go to Memphis to demo some of their joint efforts. Through Jones' intervention, their material got to the legendary Jack Clement and Bill Hall, who were running Jack and Bill Music, out of Beaumont, Texas the place where we mentioned earlier that fellow Marine George Jones played at as a child to earn extra money. Under Hall's direction, the two moved to Nashville. They had to work as deejays on radio station WENO and take other odd jobs, but the hits started to come in. They had their first cut in 1968, when another Hero of the Stage Charley Pride (USA) recorded "The Day The World Stood Still", which reached the Top 5, and followed it up with the Top 3 hit, "The Easy Part's Over", the latter earning the first of their two BMI awards. The following year, Jeannie C. Riley had a Top 40 success with "The Back Side of Dallas". In 1970, Stan Hitchcock had back-to-back hits with "Call Me Gone" and "Dixie Belle". However, that same year yet another Hero of the Stage Mel Tillis (USAF) had a Top 5 with "Heaven Everyday". In 1971, Foster and Rice racked up a slew of hits. That year, they set the then ASCAP record, receiving 5 awards. The following year, the duo had a lot of major hits that included, "Somebody Love Me", "Someone To Give My Love To", and "Love Is A Good Thing" (all by Johnny Paycheck). They got their first number one from none other than Jerry Lee Lewis when he performed their "Would You Take Another Chance On Me". Lewis also recorded "Think About It Darlin" as the flip-side of his follow-up single, "Chantilly Lace." During that year they broke their own ASCAP award record by receiving 10 awards. They went on yet again and broke that ASCAP record when they received eleven awards plus four production awards for their newly constituted production company, Farah. They had major cuts from Steve Wariner with "Easy Part's Over" in 1980, Jerry

Lee Lewis with a Top 5 single "Thirty Nine And Holding" in 1981. They also had another No. 1 hit from another Hero of the Stage Conway Twitty (USA), "Ain't She Something Else" in 1985. Jerry has had over 500 songs recorded during his career, mostly by major artists. Jerry and Bill are the most awarded songwriting team in the history of ASCAP, and hold the records for most awards in one year. They also have the distinction of having 10 songs in the billboard country music charts in one week. In 1994, he was inducted into the Nashville Songwriter's Hall of Fame and in 2007 he was inducted into the North American Country Music Association International Hall of Fame. Mr. Foster recorded an album which featured the surviving members of the original Elvis Presley Band as well as the original 1958 members of the Jordanaires. A single from that album became a number one record in Europe and as a result of the popularity of that record, Jerry toured the European continent with Roy Orbison, Jerry Lee Lewis, Mary Robbins, Jeannie C. Riley, Don Williams and Kris Kristofferson. Jerry has even worked a lot in film, including fifteen movies as well as numerous guest appearances on major television shows. He has worked with David Stratharian, Henry Thomas, Martin Landau, Jennifer O'Neil, Lindsey Wagner, Armmie Hammer, Miley Cyrus, Barry Bostwick, Vannessa Williams, and Vivica Fox to list a few. He has been featured in a number of music videos including the Grammy nominated Emmerson Drive Video "Moments" and as the preacher who baptized Stephen Baldwin in the Trace Adkins video, "Muddy Water" and Phil Vassar's video

"Bobby with an I." Jerry also played the dying grandfather in the Carrie Underwood video, "Temporary Home." He also has a book about his life and career that will be available very soon. Jerry is a true gentleman and embodies all the traits of a fine Marine and is a Hero of the Stage...

The pictures with Minnie Pearl and Ray Stevens have a very interesting story that many people have never heard. These pictures were made on the set of a television show that was filmed in 1982. The producer was "Big Daddy" Glenn Daniels, and the show was titled "Nightlife". Mr. Daniels was the founder of what is today, Country Music Television (CMT). The network was launched in March of 1982 as CMTV, and was the first country network in history, beating TNN by just one day. Jerry Fosters' voice was the first voice to be heard on the network. Glenn Daniels lifted Jerry's voice from the show that he did with Faron Young as his guest, so the first sentence on the network was "Ladies and gentlemen, here's Faron Young." The first image was Faron Young singing "Four In The Morning." Mr. Daniels was disappointed with some of his investors the way the stock was configured and was intent on building another network, so he held up the show "Nightlife" from CMTV because he planned to use it as his flagship show on his new network. Unfortunately, Mr. Daniels passed away before he could put his dream into motion and "Nightlife" was locked away in a safe somewhere. Mr. Daniels' son discovered the twenty four segments of the show and owns the properties. They have never been shown as of this day. All of the guests were very well known, including a very young Army Veteran by the name of George Strait on one of the segments. *(Jerry Foster Collection)*

HERO OF THE STAGE

Jerry Foster (USMC)

(A) Jerry Foster and Karen McVey 2010 (*Travis McVey Collection*)
(B) Jerry Foster accepting the Nashville Songwriters Lifetime
Achievement Award. (*Jerry Foster Collection*)
(C) (*Jerry Foster Collection*)

"People sleep peaceably in their beds at night only because rough men stand ready to do violence on their behalf."

George Orwell

JAMEY JOHNSON

(United States Marine)

JAMEY JOHNSON was born July 15, 1975 in Alabama. He started playing and singing Gospel music in his church when he was very young. As a child, he listened to Alabama and Hank Williams Jr. and imitated their music when he got his own guitar at ten years old. In high school, he took his guitar and some friends and went and sang on Hank Williams' grave while playing his songs on Saturday nights.

After high school, Johnson went to college for two years before dropping out and joining the United States Marine Corps Reserve in 1994. He played songs to entertain his fellow troops. Johnson also wrote music in his downtime as he was influenced by what he saw and did with the men. He spent six years serving the country before he was honorably discharged. Johnson served in Co. L, 3rd Bn, 23rd Marines as an 0341 (Mortarman) and reached the rank of Corporal.

In 2000, he moved to Nashville to start his musical career. By day, he ran a construction company and worked various jobs and he sang in clubs at night. When he attended songwriters' nights at bars he was discovered by some music executives. They hired him to sing demo tapes for various label companies. During this time, he released an album by himself that was called "They Call Me Country".

Music executives heard his talent on the demos and he got a recording contract with BNA Records in 2005. He had a hit song with "The Dollar" in the same year. Johnson got his big break when he co-wrote a song, which Trace Adkins took to the top of the charts in 2005. It was called "Honky Tonk Badonkadonk" and he received a songwriter award for it.

He seemed to be reaching star status, but then his record company dropped him and he divorced his wife. Despite being the darkest time of his life, according to him, he wrote songs which would later become part of That Lonesome Song album. UMG Nashville chairman Luke Lewis heard Johnson had worked on this album, and he offered to release it. Johnson was reluctant, because he didn't want his style changed to match a cookie cutter album for commercial success. Lewis said Johnson would have complete control, so a deal was struck. Johnson continued to work on the album while working on material for other artists.

Johnson won an ACM Award for writing George Strait's #1 song, "Give It Away" in 2007. Trace Adkins released "Ladies Love Country Boys" and "I Got My Game On" that were also co-written by Johnson. They both reached the Top 40 country charts. He has also written and co-written songs for James Otto and Joe Nichols that became hits.

In 2008, Johnson finally released the album That

Lonesome Song online. It received rave reviews for the musical talent by the LA Times, New York Times, Rolling Stone and The Washington Post. The song "In Color" reached the Top 10 list for country music. Another song "High Cost of Living" was a hit on the Top 40. The success of the album got him a deal with Mercury Records in late 2008 and The Lonesome Song was then released as a regular album.

His song "In Color" won Song of the Year at both the ACM and CMA Award shows in 2009. Johnson was nominated for five Grammy Awards in 2009 and 2010. In 2010, Johnson was the opening act for Hank Williams Jr. He also spent a lot of time in 2009 and 2010 working on an album called The Guitar Song, which is two hours' worth of music he wrote himself.

Johnson is one of the opening acts for Kid Rock's Born Free Tour. He is currently touring Willie Nelson on the "Country Throwdown Tour". For serving his Country as a Marine and protecting all of our freedoms and for continuing to support the troops he is a Hero of the Stage...

HERO OF THE STAGE

Jamey Johnson (USMC)

*"Some people spend an entire lifetime wondering
if they made a difference in the world.
The Marines don't have that problem."*

President Ronald Reagan, 1985

JOSH GRACIN

(United States Marine)

JOSHUA (JOSH) GRACIN was born October 18, 1980 and raised in Westland, Michigan. He grew up listening to R & B and country music with his family, which included four sisters. Gracin credits the Beatles, Elvis Presley and Randy Travis as his country musical influences not because he liked them so much, but because his sisters and parents listened to them all the time.

The early musical career of Gracin started as a child, when he performed in his church's Easter musical. He started listening to the radio and heard a Garth Brooks song for the first time when his favorite station changed its format to only play country music. This became his new love and he wanted to pursue country music himself. His next performance was in a talent competition where he sang a Garth Brooks song and won. Gracin also performed in local and regional talent contests while he finished school. Gracin was the only male member to perform in a group called Fairlane Youth Pops Orchestra.

In 1996, Gracin performed in a talent competition on the stage of the Grand Ole Opry. He also got to record a demo CD as part of the package. Once Gracin completed high school, he went to college briefly before joining the United States Marine Corps. As soon as his boot camp was over, he married his wife Ann Marie in 2001. Gracin was stationed in California at Camp Pendleton and worked as a supply clerk on the base. His stint in the Corps changed him. "By the time I graduated boot camp," he says, "the experience had helped define who I wanted to be and who I was going to be for the rest of my life. It's really helped prepare me for the rest of my life mentally, physically, and emotionally."

While still in the service, Gracin competed on season 2 of American Idol after encouragement from his wife and friends. He took fourth place, however because of his prior commitment to the Marine Corps, Josh was not able to participate in the lucrative American Idol Finalists tour of American venues. Gracin was instead sent on a very important recruiting tour making appearances at special events around the United States to promote the United States Marines. After completing his fourth year of service, he was honorably discharged in September 2004. He signed a contract with Lyric Street Records that same year.

His first album, which was self -titled, was released in 2004. Three hits came from that album and included "I Want to Live", Stay With Me (Brass Bed)" and "Nothin' to Lose". "Nothin' to Lose" hit #1 on the country charts while the other two songs cracked the Top 5.

Gracin's second album called "We Weren't Crazy" was released in 2008. Songs from that album were popular, but not chart toppers. Those songs included "Favorite State of Mind", "Unbelievable" and "We Weren't Crazy". Lyric Street Records did not renew Gracin's contract after those releases.

When he was without a label to back him, Gracin wrote a song titled "Enough" and posted it on his MySpace page in 2009. The song earned a lot of praise from his fans and Gracin believed it was a turning point in his career. He started writing more music and developed a style he was happy with.

Gracin then signed with Average Joe Entertainment in 2010. He released a song called "Cover Girl" but it was not attached to an album project, just like his song "Enough". A new album is scheduled for release in 2011 and has yet to be named.

Gracin lives in Nashville with his wife and four children. Josh has brought great credit upon himself and the United States Marine Corps during and after his service. He continues to exemplify the Honor, Courage, and Commitment values of a Marine and shows his support of our men and women in the military and he is a Hero of the Stage...

American Idol (Fox) season 2
January 21 - May 21, 2003
Shown: "Final 6" Clockwise from top: Joshua Gracin,
Ruben Studdard, Carmen Rasmusen, Kimberley Locke,
Lashundra "Trenyce" Cobbins, Clay Aiken. *(Fox/Photofest)*

HERO OF THE STAGE

Josh Gracin (USMC)

American Idol (Fox) season 2
January 21 - May 21, 2003
Shown: finalists Corey Clark, Joshua Gracin *(Fox/Photofest)*

JASON MICHAEL CARROLL

(United States Marine)

JASON MICHAEL CARROLL was born June 13, 1978 in Houston, Texas to a strict preacher's family and grew up in North Carolina. As a child, secular music was not allowed in the Carroll household or in the car. When he went to his friend's houses, he was eager to find a radio and listen to country and rock and roll music. Carroll developed a love of music despite his father's wishes however, and often snuck off to buy tapes when he got the chance. He was punished by his father when he found Billy Ray Cyrus' "Achy Breaky Heart" recording in his room. It didn't stop him from wanting to be a musician and singer though.

Carroll sang in church and wrote songs through school. In high school, he worked in a garage that only played country music on the radio and it inspired Carroll. He practiced in secret, perfecting his talent. Carroll also earned his Eagle, Globe and Anchor and became a United States Marine and served in the Reserves.

He decided to sign up for a karaoke contest at a radio station in 2004. He won the contest and earned a spot singing for a band called Chasin' Country. While singing in clubs and bars, he got some recognition for his singing and writing talent.

The band and Carroll parted ways over a disagreement over a regular performance. During this time, his mother also signed him up for a contest, which he also won in Raleigh. In the summer of 2005, he was singing in bars and clubs in Nashville as a solo act. Music executives discovered him and he was signed to a record deal with Arista.

His first album was called "Waitin' in the Country" and produced "Alyssa Lies" and "Livin' Our Love Song" which both reached the Top 6 on the music charts. The album debuted at the #1 spot due to the songs' popularity before the album was released. Carroll was named Top New Country Artist for the year 2007.

His second album called "Growing Up Is Getting Old" was released by Arista Nashville in 2009. He had a hit with "Where I'm From". No other songs reached popular status from the album, so he and Arista did not renew their contract.

In 2010, he signed an exclusive deal with QuarterBack/ Grass Roots/Cracker Barrel to produce an album called "Numbers". It was released in 2011 and only sold through Cracker Barrel stores.

Carroll has opened for Alan Jackson, Brooks and Dunn and Trace Adkins. In 2008, he also worked with Carrie Underwood and Martina McBride on their tours. Carroll often performs special shows for Marines and their families around the country. He makes sure to take time to sign autographs and let them know they are appreciated. At one event where over 150 Marines were set to ship out Carroll said, "It was really nice to be able to give back to the Marines who give us so much. Their bags were packed, their families were there; it was so emotional. Whenever I see someone in uniform, at the airport or somewhere else, I make it a point, even go out of my way, to go over and thank them for their service. They give me the freedom to do what I do." Jason Michael Carroll we thank you for what you do and for your service as a United States Marine and you are a Hero of the Stage...

HERO OF THE STAGE

Jason Michael Carroll (USMC)

PART TWO

UNITED STATES ARMY

Kris Kristofferson

George Strait

Charley Pride

Craig Morgan

John Conlee

Keni Thomas

Rockie Lynne

Sonny James

Ryan Weaver

Tom T. Hall

*"A better world shall emerge based on faith
and understanding"*

General Douglas MacArthur

KRIS KRISTOFFERSON

(United States Army)

KRIS KRISTOFFERSON was born June 22, 1936 in Brownsville, Texas. His family was a military family, so Kris is what we would call a military brat and they moved around frequently while he was a child. His father was an Air Force Major General and he pushed Kris toward a military career. It is also interesting to note that Kris' paternal grandfather was an officer in the Swedish Army. Kristofferson graduated from high school in California and then went on to college. He was a student at Pomona College and excelled at sports. He received a degree in literature in 1958. Kristofferson went on to Study at Oxford on a Rhodes Scholarship. It was over in England when he began to write music. In 1960, he graduated with another literature degree.

After he earned his degrees, Kristofferson joined the United States Army. His Army service included becoming a Ranger and a helicopter pilot. In the 1960s, he was stationed in Alabama, and then sent overseas to West Germany as a member of the 8th Infantry Division. Kristofferson formed a band in Germany and started playing music again. He earned the rank of Captain while serving the country. His brother Kraigher Kristofferson is like Kris, a veteran of the Armed Forces. Kraigher was a Navy fighter pilot and served in the Vietnam War. Kris is quoted as saying, "I grew up in a time when people believed in duty, honor and country. My grandfathers were both officers. My father was a General in the Air Force. My brother and I both served. I've always felt a kinship with soldiers; I think it's possible to support the warrior and be against the war."

Living in Tennessee, I also learned that a couple of years after he got out of the Army Kristofferson joined the Tennessee National Guard and flew helicopters.

Once he was honorably discharged from military service in 1965, he was asked to teach English Literature at West Point. He originally signed up for the deal, but then he declined only two weeks before classes were to begin. He chose to pursue a career in music instead and packed his bags and headed out for Nashville.

The first job he held was as a floor sweeper for Columbia Studios. While working this job, he met Johnny Cash and handed him some songs. They were never recorded, but it kept Kristofferson trying. Kristofferson also got to see Bob Dylan record his famous song, "Blonde on Blonde" in 1966.

Kristofferson split his time between trying to make it in Nashville and working as a pilot for the petroleum industry. While he was on standby as a pilot, he worked on songs. Over the weekends, he would sweep floors and pitch his various songs to music executives. It took a few years before any of Kristofferson's songs made the charts.

The first songs that made the charts were "Jody and the Kid", "From the Bottle to the Bottom", "Once More With Feeling" and "Me and Bobby McGee". Kristofferson got his break not for his singing, but for his flying skills. His helicopter training more than once served him well. In a remarkable incident and a Music City true to life legend, he met up with Johnny Cash again when he was tired of being rebuffed. Instead of waiting for Cash to listen to his songs, he took his helicopter and landed it in his yard and handed him the recording. Cash recognized Kristofferson and gave his song another chance. He agreed to listen to a tune called "Sunday Morning Coming Down". Johnny Cash, before he was known as the "Man In Black", he was known as the "Man In Blue" being a veteran himself of the United States Air Force. I have often thought it would be a great thing if the Country Music Hall of Fame would have an exhibit of all the Heroes of the Stage. For the premier of such an exhibit I could see Kris and a bunch of them land in a helicopter in front of the Hall of Fame to attend the opening. How many of us would love to see something as spectacular as that? It would not only show that bond between Country Artists but between Veterans as well.

Later, Cash introduced Kristofferson to the stage at the Newport Folk Festival. After that, Kristofferson got a record deal in 1970 with Monument. His first album was called "Kristofferson" and it produced no hits and was not a commercial success. It was re-titled "Me & Bobby McGee" the next year and re-released, and then it became a hit.

Other songs he wrote were becoming bigger hits. These songs included Waylon Jennings singing "The Taker", Johnny Cash singing "Sunday Morning Coming Down" and Ray Price with "For the Good Times". It turned out that Ray Price took "For The Good Times" to the top of the charts and it earned him a Song of the Year in 1970 from the AMC Awards. Johnny Cash's "Sunday Morning" won Song of the Year the same year but by the CMA Awards. Kristofferson won two song of the year awards within the same year.

Other singers were taking Kristofferson songs to the top of the charts. These artists included Janis Joplin (who briefly dated Kristofferson), Bobby Bare, Jerry Lee Lewis and Patti Page.

Besides music, Kristofferson had a love of acting. He took a leave from music and went on to star in some low budget movies. His other big break in acting came when he starred with Barbra Streisand in A Star is Born. He received a Golden Globe Award in the Best Actor category for his role.

In 1971, Kristofferson won a Grammy Award for writing the song "Help Me Make it Through the Night" which was sung by Sammi Smith. That song also earned a Grammy for Smith, a CMA Award for Single of the Year and Best Female Performance. In the same year, Janis Joplin recorded a pop version of the song "Me and Bobby McGee" and took it to #1.

Kristofferson married another singer by the name of Rita Coolidge. They were married from 1973 until 1980 and recorded several albums of duets together. These collaborations earned them two Grammy Awards.

During the 1970s and 1980s, Kristofferson worked with Willie Nelson, Dolly Parton, Brenda Lee and many others on various albums. None were a huge success until he formed the group The Highwaymen. This quartet included Willie Nelson, Johnny Cash and Waylon Jennings. Their album of the name Lost Highwaymen earned an ACM in 1985 for the song, "Lost Highwaymen". The Lost Highwaymen 2 was released in 1990.

Kristofferson was voted in to the Nashville Songwriters Hall of Fame in 1977. He was elected in to the Songwriters Hall of Fame in 1985. In 2002, he was named Veteran of the Year by the American Veteran Awards. In 2004, he was inducted in to the Country Music Hall of Fame.

In 2009, Kristofferson released an album called "Closer to the Bone". The album did not produce any hits, but it was recognized as being beautiful work. Kristofferson continues to tour and promote his work with various friends. He is also a social activist and fights for veteran's rights.

Kristofferson has been married three times and has eight children. Mr. Kristofferson is a living legend and widely respected in the Veteran community. He served his Country well in so many ways and continues to serve her even today and he is a Hero of the Stage...

The Highwaymen (ca. 1985)
Shown (l-r): Willie Nelson, Waylon Jennings,
Kris Kristofferson, Johnny Cash

Cisco Pike (1972)Directed by Bill L. Norton…
Shown from left: Kris Kristofferson/United States Army Veteran
(as Cisco Pike), Gene Hackman/U.S. Marine Veteran
(as Sergeant Leo Holland) *(Photo Credit: Columbia Pictures/Photofest)*

The Johnny Cash Christmas Show (December 6, 1978)
shown: Johnny Cash, June Carter Cash, Rita Coolidge,
Kris Kristofferson

"Tell the truth. Sing with Passion.
Work with Laughter. Love with heart.
'Cause that's all that matters in the end."

Kris Kristofferson

HERO OF THE STAGE

Kris Kristofferson (U.S. Army)

"The safest place in Korea was right behind a platoon of Marines. Lord how they could fight."

Major General Frank Lowe, U.S. Army

GEORGE STRAIT

(United States Army)

GEORGE HARVEY STRAIT was born May 18, 1952 in Poteet, Texas just south of San Antonio, and grew up in the nearby town of Big Wells, Texas. His dad was a junior high school math teacher who also owned and operated a 2,000 acre cattle ranch that had been in the Strait family for nearly 100 years. The family would work the ranch on the weekends and in the summers. When George was just a child his mother left the family, taking her daughter but leaving behind George and his brother John Jr. Strait started his music career in rock and roll, while he was in high school. He sang rock with a band for fun until he heard the likes of Hank Williams, George Jones and Merle Haggard and other country artists at small town fairs and concerts in Texas. His beginnings were humble, just like the person he is, despite being named the King of Country and having more #1 hits than any other person on the planet in any musical genre.

Strait had intentions of getting a college education, but dropped out a few months after registering. Instead, Strait eloped with his wife Norma in December of 1971. That same year, he signed up for the US Army, where he really became interested in singing country music. Strait's military assignment took him to Hawaii, where he was stationed at Schofield Barracks with the 25th Infantry. There was an Army band called Rambling Country that Strait joined and performed in. Strait was honorably discharged in 1975 after serving four years.

Once leaving the military life behind, Strait registered at Texas State University and joined a band called Stoney Ridge. He found the band by spotting an ad posted for the group because they were in need of a lead singer (and he was in need of a new band). The band renamed themselves Ace in the Hole once Strait came on board with them. They played at regional bars and honky tonks, but never had luck at breaking out in to a larger audience than their regional fans for the first years. They recorded a song with D label records, but the song never got airtime or became a hit.

Strait continued to play in bars at night and worked the family cattle ranch during the day. His break didn't come until the manager of one of the bars he played at invited his friends – who happened to be executives at MCA Records – to come and listen to Strait and Ace in the Hole. Strait had only sung a few songs before they realized he had incredible talent and needed to get him on board. MCA and Strait signed an agreement in 1980 and his first record called "Strait Country" was released the next year.

"Strait Country" produced a few top 40 hits, such as

"Unwound" and "If You're Thinking You Want a Stranger". Strait went right back to work and released his second album called "Strait From the Heart" in 1982. That record produced his first #1 song, "Fool Hearted Memory". It also contained one of the songs that most people know Strait by, "Amarillo By Morning" which is a rodeo song about lost love, cattle and living on the road – a true cowboy anthem.

The 1980s proved to be successful as Strait had 17 #1 songs in the decade. He also released several more albums, some of which went to the #1 spot on the charts. Strait ended the year by winning the CMA Entertainer of the Year in 1989 and again in 1990.

Despite his enormous leap to success, Strait and his family managed to stay out of trouble and out of the spotlight. The 70s and 80s saw other country stars go deep in to alcoholism, drugs and cancel shows, yet Strait managed to keep his tour dates and stay clean. The only incident where he was in the spotlight was after his 13 year old daughter Jennifer was killed in a car accident in 1986. Strait took time off from recording music and touring, but he got back in to the industry a short time later without any repercussions.

In 1992, Strait branched out in to the world of show business and was the main character in Warner Bros. movie called, "Pure Country". This movie produced a soundtrack that raced up the charts and produced several hit songs, including "Heartland", "I Cross My Heart" and "When Did You Stop Loving Me". The movie was not a huge box office hit, but the soundtrack of the same name became his biggest selling album to date. A sequel to "Pure Country" was filmed in 2009, but had a limited release and went to DVD not long after. Strait also appeared in the 1982 movie called the Soldier and in Grand Champion, which was filmed in 2002.

The 1990s saw Strait earn 17 #1 songs, including "Write This Down", "What Do You Say to That" and "Meanwhile". He produced several chart topping albums, while maintaining hits on the billboard charts. Strait was one of the biggest touring acts in the 1990s.

The George Strait Country Music Festival started in 1997 with Strait headlining the tour and allowing other, lesser known acts (at the time) to open for him. Those acts included Tim McGraw, Faith Hill, Kenny Chesney, the Dixie Chicks and Alan Jackson – all of which are huge stars on their own now. This festival was later voted the most important tour in country music history, despite only playing 20 or so shows a year. It also managed to be the 9th highest grossing tour in 1998, even with such small numbers. The Festival only had a limited amount of shows, but they were played in arenas and areas where tens of thousands of fans could buy tickets.

An interesting fact with Strait's career is that he has had a song on the Billboard every week since his first album debuted in 1981. That's 30 years of having at least one song somewhere in the top 100. No other artist can come close to that feat in rock, rap or hip hop.

Strait has racked up many awards and honors as a singer, including 22 CMA (Country Music Association) Awards. He holds the record for most nominations for the CMAs and the ACMs (Academy of Country Music). Strait was voted the biggest country music artist for the last twenty five years by Billboard magazine in 2010.

While Strait is a very private man, there are little details released about his private life. Strait lives with his wife in San Antonio, is a huge fan of the NBA team, the San Antonio Spurs and is a spokesman for a Chevy Dealership in Texas. He and his wife also have a son, George Strait, Jr., known as "Bubba" who was born in 1982, and rides the rodeo circuit.

Strait was inducted in to the Country Music Hall of Fame in 2006. He said he refuses to retire and will keep singing and performing, as long as he is able. He and his wife remain humble people and donate a lot of time and money to charity, especially the foundation set up in memory of his late daughter. This foundation is called the Jenifer Lynn Strait Foundation, which donates money to children's charities. Georges Strait may be the King of Country but he was also willing to serve his Country as a soldier in the United States Army and for that and so much more he is definitely one of the Heroes of the Stage...

HERO OF THE STAGE

George Strait (U.S. Army)

"Don't tell me the sky is the limit when there are foot prints on the moon."

Unknown

CHARLEY PRIDE

(United States Army)

CHARLEY FRANK PRIDE was born on March 18th, 1938, one of eleven children in Sledge, Mississippi. His parents were poor sharecroppers. He unofficially started his music career as a baseball player in the Negro American League with the Memphis Red Sox, singing and playing guitar on the team bus between ballparks. He was self-taught on a guitar bought at the age of 14 from Sears Roebuck. Charley would also join various bands on stage as the team traveled the country.

Though Charley loved music, one of his life-long dreams was to become a professional baseball player. He was a pitcher for the Memphis Red Sox in 1952 and he was a good pitcher. In 1953, he signed with the Boise Yankees, the Class C farm team of the New York Yankees. During that season, an injury caused him to lose the "mustard" on his fastball, and he was sent to the Yankees' Class D team in Fond du Lac, Wisconsin. Later that season while in the Negro Leagues he played with the Louisville Clippers, he and another player (Jesse Mitchell), were traded to the Birmingham Black Barons for a team bus. Pride mused in his 1994 autobiography, "Jesse and I may have the distinction of being the only players in history to be traded for a used motor vehicle."

Charley served two years in the United States Army and after being honorably discharged, he tried to return to baseball. Though still somewhat hindered to an injury to his throwing arm, he had tryouts with the California Angels and the New York Mets, but was not signed by either team. When it became apparent that he was not going to be a professional baseball player he started to pursue his music career.

During a trip to Nashville, Pride was introduced to producer, Jack Clement, who gave him several songs to learn. When Clement heard Pride's renditions, he immediately asked the fledgling singer if he could cut two songs in a two hour recording session. The result in about 3 months was a two-song demo that landed him a recording contract with RCA Records after Chet Atkins liked what he heard. His first single hit the airwaves in January of 1966 and just like that his star was on the rise. His race was kept hidden from the fans through the release of his first three singles. Making one of his first big public appearances at a show in Detroit, Pride stepped on stage and was greeted with loud applause, which got lower and lower in volume until near silence as most of the audience began to make the realization that he was a black country singer. But Pride's music prevailed and, after the show, he was besieged with autograph seekers.

Soon after the release of "Snakes Crawl at Night", Charley released another single called "Before I Met You". Soon after, his third single, "Just Between You and Me", was released. This song was what finally brought Charley Pride his success on the Country charts. Then he won a Grammy Award for the song the next year.

In 1971, Charley would release what would become his biggest hit of all time "Kiss an Angel Good Mornin'", a million-selling crossover single that helped him land the Country Music Association's prestigious Entertainer of the Year award, as well as Top Male Vocalist. He won CMA's Top Male Vocalist award again in 1972. He was the first artist to win back-to back male vocalist trophies. His RCA singles routinely reached the Top 10 through 1984.

Other memorable Pride standards include "Is Anybody Goin' To San Antone?","I'm So Afraid of Losing You Again," "Mississippi Cotton Picking Delta Town," "Someone Loves You Honey," "When I Stop Leaving I'll be Gone," "Burgers and Fries," and "You're So Good When You're Bad," to name but a few. His moving performances of Hank Williams' classics "Kaw-Liga" and "Honky Tonk Blues" on his number 1 album, "There's a Little Bit of Hank in Me", was also certified Gold.

Over the past thirty years, Pride has remained one of the Top 20 best-selling country artists of all-time. His incredible legacy includes 36 #1 hit singles, over 70 million albums sold, 31 gold and 4 platinum albums - including one quadruple platinum. On RCA Records, Charley Pride is second in sales only to Elvis Presley. Charley has also sung the National Anthem at 5 World Series games.

By the mid- 1980s, Pride's prowess in business was beginning to equal that of his recording career. During this period, he split his time between his music and his business activities in banking, broadcasting and real estate. He is the major stockholder in the largest minority owned bank in Texas, the First Texas Bank. He has owned four diverse radio stations and extensive real estate holdings across the country, including the Charley Pride Theater in Branson, Mo. Pride stays actively involved in the music industry through his publishing company, The Pride Group, and his production company. Charley is also an investor in his favorite team the Texas Rangers.

In 1994, Charley released his autobiography, Pride: The Charley Pride Story (published by William Morrow). Aside from detailing great moments of his amazing career and journeyman stint as a ballplayer, Pride: is an often moving, sometimes hilarious tale of his almost improbable dream come true and journey to the top of the charts. In his own words, Charley recalls his hardscrabble childhood, his enduring marriage, the thrill of his biggest hit – a double into the outfield gap off Hall of Famer Warren Spahn - and his first singing engagement in a Montana bar that eventually led to a career as the first and only African-American superstar in country music. Through it all, we are reminded that "The Pride of Country Music" remains one of the great legends in popular music - and that he is still going strong.

On May 1, 1993, Pride accepted a long-standing invitation to join the Grand Ole Opry, 26 years after he first played there as a guest, the first African-American in its over 70 year history. In June 1994, Pride was honored by the Academy Of Country Music with its prestigious Pioneer Award. In January 1996, Charley Pride was honored with a Trumpet Award by Turner Broadcasting, marking outstanding African-American Achievement. In between, his "Roll On Mississippi" was considered as the official song of his home state, a stretch of Mississippi highway was named for him, and he headlined a special Christmas performance for President and Mrs. Clinton at the White House.

In July 1999, Charley received his very own star on the Hollywood Walk of Fame. On October 4, 2000, Charley was honored with the highest country music award, he was inducted into the Country Music Hall of Fame. Charley wept when his name was announced by Hall of Famer, Brenda Lee. And just in case music should leave his blood, Pride continues to work out annually with baseball's Texas Rangers. When not touring extensively world-wide or recording music, Pride can often be found pursuing another love, one at which he also excels - golf. Charley Pride met the love of his life, Rozene, while playing baseball in Memphis. They have raised two sons, Kraig and Dion, as well as a daughter, Angela. They also en-joy their grandsons, Carlton and Malachi in Dallas, Texas, where their family resides. Pride continues his illustri-ous career with the release of "Comfort of Her Wings" on

Music City Records. The album shows that Charley has not slowed down and proves his voice is as good, if not better than ever. Professional Athlete, Soldier, Legendary Entertainer and savvy Businessman; Charley Pride has definitely earned his place as a Hero of the Stage...

HERO OF THE STAGE

Charley Pride (U.S. Army)

"I think Charley Pride has been one of the best things to happen to country music, to prove it belongs to everybody."

Loretta Lynn

CRAIG MORGAN

Dod photo by: Amy K. Mitchell

(United States Army)

CRAIG MORGAN GREER was born July 17, 1964 in Kingston Springs, Tennessee. He became an emergency medical technician (EMT) at the age of only 18. He later enlisted in the United States Army and was even stationed in South Korea. When Craig was in Korea he started entering singing and songwriting contests and winning them. He then thought he might have a chance at a music career, but it wasn't until years later that he actually pursued it. Craig spent more than ten years on active duty in the United States Army as a Fire Support Specialist earning the rank of Staff Sergeant. He served in the 101st and 82nd Airborne Divisions before actually launching his music career. He holds Airborne, Jumpmaster, and Air Assault qualifications. In 1989, he saw combat in Operation Just Cause in Panama, during which the United States overthrew the dictator Manuel Noriega.

Craig left the Army in 1996, but he continued to serve by performing for the troops in the Middle East and elsewhere as a volunteer for the USO and that is work he continues today. As I write this line it is February 3rd, 2011 and his website at www.craigmorgan.com is letting everyone know Craig is currently in Iraq on the NOT ALONE tour, his ninth overseas visit to our US troops stationed abroad.

It seems like Craig couldn't get that ole green blood out of him and in August of 2001 he enlisted in the Army Reserve in spectacular style. He took a parachute jump along with members of the Army's Golden Knights parachute team at Fort Campbell, Kentucky. After his landing, he was sworn in as a member of the Nashville based 86 1st Quartermaster Company. Like all members of the Army Reserve, he continued his own career but devoted weekends to drill with his unit in the Army. He served as a Staff Sergeant, the rank he left active duty, and trained as an automated supply specialist. Morgan told Lee Elder in the Army Reserve Magazine, "I'm real proud of the Army. That's why I'm back." He added, "It looks like I'm going to have to cut my hair."

After leaving the Army in 1996, Craig returned to Tennessee and did work in various jobs such as a construction worker, as a security guard and even as a deputy sheriff. He continued pursuing his music career and eventually got a job in Nashville singing demo songs for other songwriters and music publishing companies. It was while singing these demos that he was signed with Atlantic Records, where he released his self-titled album in 2000. Atlantic Records shut down soon after that, and Craig was without a label until

2003, where he signed with the independent label Broken Bow Records.

He then released "I Love It" in 2003, a single from the album, "Almost Home," and it hit the country Top 10 and won a Songwriter Achievement Award from the Nashville Songwriters Association. To this, Craig replied, "Oh, God Yes! I do love the G Award from the Nashville Songwriters Association. In Country Standard Time, Jeffery B. Renz wrote, "His singing is well suited to the material, especially when he keeps it country." Rick Cohoon of Allmusic gave "I Love It" four stars out of five, saying that Morgan's songwriting was "well-crafted" and that his service in the Army justified the patriotic themes of "God, Family and Country". By 2004, the album had sold more than 300,000 copies, and its success was cited as the beginning of a new wave of commercial success among independently-signed country music artists.

In 2005, Craig released his third album "My Kind of Livin'" which brought him his first No. 1 "That's What I Love About Sunday." The song stayed on top of the charts for four straight weeks, and by years end, became the most played song of 2005. Other songs from the same album included fan-favorite "Redneck Yacht Club" and "I Got You." The album also earned the Army Veteran his first Gold Album, having sold over 500,000 copies. "Redneck Yacht Club" itself received a gold single certification for 500,000 music downloads. In People, Ralph Novak noted that Morgan "sings apologetically about his guns, collard greens, rodeos and 'a trailer with a concrete donkey in the yard,'" and commented that this honest, very down-home presentation was part of Morgan's success: the album is "one terrific, old fashioned country CD."

Craig released "Little Bit of Life" in late 2006, which brought him two more Top 10 songs with the title cut (No. 7) and "International Harvester," which peaked at No. 10. The song "Tough" made it as high as No. 11.

In February 2008, Craig announced he was leaving Broken Bow for BNA Nashville. His first album for the label was released in October, entitled "That's Why". The debut single was "Love Remembers," another Morgan co-write. Also in September of 2008, while performing for the troops at Ft. Bragg, North Carolina (one of the many places he had been stationed during his Army service) Craig was surprised by friend and Opry member Jon Conlee. It was during this surprise visit that Conlee invited Craig to join the Grand Ole Opry. To this, Craig replied, "Oh, God Yes! I do love the Grand Ole Opry! And I gotta tell you, it's cool to be invited right here." His formal induction into the Opry took place on Saturday October 25, 2008. Backstage that night at the Opry, Craig told the story of how at 12 years old, he went on a field trip to a Nashville historic site, and sang the "Star Spangled Banner." Afterwards, he was approached by a woman who told him, "Young man, you're going to be a famous country singer one day." That woman was none other than Minnie Pearl. Then, he pointed out that Saturday was Minnie Pearl's birthday...

As stated earlier, his first album for BNA Records a division of Sony BMG Nashville was That's Why. It's first single, "Love Remembers" became his sixth top ten hit by early 2009, but follow-up "God Must Really Love Me" peaked at 26. In October of 2009, the music video for "God Must Really Love Me" won Video of the Year from the Inspirational Country Music Awards. In early 2010, "This Ain't Nothin" was released as the album's fourth single and it became a top 20 country hit by year's end. His last single for BNA, "Still a Little Chicken Left on That Bone", was released in October 2010. The song peaked at number 37 on the country music charts in January 2011. A month later, Craig left the label.

Craig recently - as I'm writing this chapter about him - proved himself yet again as a true Hero by rescuing a family from a burning house. During what he thought would be a quiet Sunday afternoon after returning from a string of tour dates to his hometown of Dickson, Tennessee witnessed a house fire and sprang into action. Putting his skills as a former EMT, Soldier and Deputy Sheriff to work, Craig raced to the scene and into the smoke-filled house to rescue two young children still inside. When the fire trucks arrived, the firefighters handed him a hose to help dampen the flames. Thanks to the singer's quick reaction and disregard for his own well-being, the home suffered relatively minor damage and the two young children made it out safely.

Craig also has a very successful TV series on the Outdoor Channel titled "Craig Morgan-All Access Outdoors" that debuted in July of 2010. Every Saturday at 11am (eastern), All Access Outdoors will follow Craig traveling across North America while hunting for big game and riding motocross.

Each week he will be joined by special guests such as motocross celebrities, professional athletes and other country music artists.

Craig is married to wife Karen and has four children: a daughter, Alex, and sons Kyle, Jerry, and Wyatt. One hobby that he shares with his children is racing dirt bikes, and he maintains a track at his home where they can ride.

In an interview in Soldiers magazine in 2006, Craig had this advice for soldiers who were deployed around the world, "Keep your head up and be proud of who you are and what you're doing. The men and women of the armed forces need to know that America supports them." He is also grateful for the support that he gets from his fans; he told an interviewer in CountryMusic.About.com, "I'm saddened that some of us in the industry do forget that sometimes, the fans truly are to be thanked for their support. I'm grateful to be here." Craig Morgan has served his Country bravely and with honor and continues to serve by his unwavering support of the men and women who serve our Nation. As they say "Rangers lead the way" and Craig certainly leads the way when it comes to taking the time to visit and entertain our brave men and women in uniform. Craig Morgan is a Hero of the Stage...

Bragg jumpmaster-turned-country-music-star Craig Morgan poses with Staff Sgt. Victor Sorrento and other soldiers of the United States Forces - Iraq 'Roughriders,' a convoy operations team, following a performance at Camp Victory, Iraq. *Photo by: Sgt. A.M. LaVey*

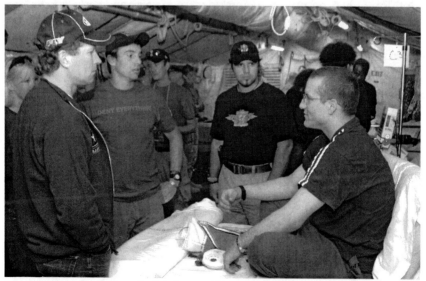

Pfc. Woodrow Carter, 3rd Infantry Division, gets a surprise visit from country singers Craig Morgan, Keni Thomas and Mark Wills at the Camp Arifjan Expeditionary Medical Facility Kuwait, Dec. 15, 2005. *Photo by: PFC Michael Noggle*

Sgt. Tobi D. Nelson, an automated logistic specialist and her husband, Sgt. 1st Class Matthew Nelson, a senior human resources non-commissioned officer, both XVIII Airborne Corps soldiers supporting U.S. Forces - Iraq, meet with Craig Morgan, a country musician after a concert at Camp Victory, Iraq. *Photo by: Sgt. A.M. LaVey*

HERO OF THE STAGE

Craig Morgan (U.S. Army)

JOHN CONLEE

(United States Army)

Country artist John Conlee (far right in glasses) is joined by his son, Johnny, while singing his hit song "Rose Colored Glasses." Johnny joined the Marines in 2004, went to Fallujah in Iraq twice and was awarded the Purple Heart for injuries received during combat. *Photo Credit: Steve Elliott (us.army.mil)*

JOHN CONLEE was born August 11th, 1946 in Versailles, Kentucky on a tobacco farm. He took up the guitar at an early age and was already performing on local radio by age ten. He went to also sing with the town barbershop chorus and sang high tenor, but didn't take up music as a career until later on, instead he became a licensed mortician. John also enlisted in the Kentucky Army National Guard in the early seventies. He is quoted as saying in an interview on the official homepage of the United States Army at the Warrior Family Support Center in 2010, "I was in the Kentucky Army National Guard in the Vietnam era in 1973. While I did not go to Vietnam, I remember the treatment of our veterans during that era. It was sorry and sad. This country has learned a lesson since then, or at least I hope it has," Conlee added. "I just want to do everything I can to keep that feeling alive. What happened before was wrong, but we can make it up to our veterans today."

Conlee has also seen the military on a more personal

note through the eyes of his son. "My son, Johnny, went in the Marines in 2004," Conlee said. "He went to fight in Fallujah in Iraq twice and was injured and was awarded the Purple Heart. That was the genesis for me to pay much more attention to what is going on."

John also worked as a disc jockey at numerous area radio stations, and made important industry connections via that area when he moved to Nashville in 1971. He signed to ABC Records in 1976 and charted for the first time in 1978 with "Rose Colored Glasses," a number 5 hit on the Billboard Hot Country Singles (now Hot Country Songs) charts, as well as the title track to his 1978 debut album. This album would go on to produce his first two Number One hits in "Lady Lay Down" and "Backside of Thirty."

Born and raised on the farm, Jon grew up a farmer's life by plowing fields, slopping hogs, harvesting grain, raising tobacco, and tending cattle. He began his crusade to save the family farm system years ago, performing at a concert in Omaha Nebraska in June of 1985 as a benefit for the National Farmers Organization. When another Heroes of the Stage alumni fellow veteran Willie Nelson announced his plans for the Farm Aid concerts, John called and offered his services. John has since been a part of 9 Farm Aid concerts, which have raised over 13 million dollars to aid the family farmer. Jon is quoted as saying on his website , "I certainly didn't help organize the entertainers and the concerts for the publicity. I wanted to help bring attention to the crisis affecting this nation's family farms. With the help of Willie and others, we brought the family problems to the forefront and some changes began to take place. I'm not a radical or a rebel," Conlee continues, "but I will stand up and speak my mind on issues that I feel affect me, my family and others, and the farm crisis was, and remains, one of those issues."

Conlee said his songs are about the lives of the everyday middle class, hardworking people, and those who've been unable to attain even that level of economic ease. "There are more of us ordinary folks than anybody else," Conlee said.

This extraordinary hero also raised more than $140,000 for Feed the Children one dollar at a time for the charity from the dollar bills tossed on the stage when he sings his 1983 hit version of "Busted".

John stated in an interview at Fort Sam Houston, "I've been concentrating on the wounded warriors in general the past several years." He has also a released a DVD titled "They Also Serve." The DVD is a tribute to the Family and friends of those serving in the Armed Forces, and it portrays the lives of Families and friends dealing with loved ones affected by current U.S. military actions.

"Their sacrifice now is so great," Conlee said. "Back in the 70s, there was a draft. Now this is an all-volunteer military, and that makes even more of a difference."

Unlike many artists today, there are several aspects of John Conlee's career that have remained constant. His career has been managed from the beginning by Dave Roberts and all his records have been produced by Bud Logan. In the entertainment world where artists change managers, agents and producers almost as often as they change their socks, John Conlee has not tampered with success. He has remained loyal and constant with the people who have helped him from the beginning – which tells you quite a bit about the man with the rose colored glasses.

Overall, there have been 29 single releases throughout the years with 26 of them charting in the top 20 or better. Eight of those 26 have reached the coveted No. 1 spot on the national country charts. Jon has also been a proud member of the Grand Ole Opry since 1981.

John Conlee is a lot like the songs of which he sings. He lives a domestic life with his wife Gale and three children, Rebecca, Jessica and Johnny. During the past two decades, John Conlee has achieved a level of success that he has sustained by simply being himself and by making records that the listening public can relate to. He is a gifted entertainer, but he's not into the glitz and hype of the entertainment world. He'd rather spend his "off the road" time working on his 32 acre farm outside of Nashville, or engaging in his woodworking and gun-smithing hobbies. John says, "There is no glamour to it. Woodworking, gun-smithing or driving a tractor requires getting grease or varnish all over you. Its dirty work, but I like it." John is a very humble man that has a huge heart for the right causes in life. John is a big supporter of the men and women in the military and has also raised awareness of the sacrifices the families and loved ones have to make for those that serve as well. For all of this and more John Conlee is a Hero of the Stage...

Country artist John Conlee signs a DVD for Spc. Benjamin Olsen after he and his band performed six of his hit songs at the Warrior and Family Support Center Aug. 27, 2010. *Photo Credit: Steve Elliott (us.army.mil)*

HERO OF THE STAGE

Photo by Steve Elliott(us.army.mil)

John Conlee (U.S. Army)

"The true soldier fights not because he hates what is in front of him, but because he loves what is behind him."

G.K. Chesterton

KENI THOMAS

(Keni Thomas Collection)

(United States Army)

KENI THOMAS enlisted in the United States Army in 1991. Prior to joining the Army, he attended the University of Florida. After completion of the Airborne school and the Ranger Indoctrination program, he was assigned to B Company 3rd Ranger Battalion of the 75th Ranger Regiment where he subsequently earned his Ranger Tab. In the summer of 1993, Sergeant Thomas and B Company were deployed to Mogadishu, Somalia as part of a special operations package called Task Force Ranger.

Once deployed to Somalia, Task Force Ranger's primary mission was to locate and capture the criminal warlord Mohammed Farrah Aideed. On October 3, 1993, Thomas and his fellow Rangers distinguished themselves in an eighteen hour fire fight that would later be recounted in the highly successful book and movie "Blackhawk Down". Tragically, nineteen Americans died and 78 were wounded in the worst urban combat seen at that time by US troops since WWII.

With a promotion to Staff Sergeant, Keni stayed in the

Army for three additional years as an assistant team leader for a six man Ranger reconnaissance team. His military decorations and achievements include the Bronze Star for Valor and the Combat Infantry Badge. He earned his master parachutist rating with over 380 military free fall jumps, the British and Belgian parachute wings. He completed the Special Forces Combat Diver course, Pathfinder School, HALO (High Altitude Low Opening) School, and Cold Weather Mountaineering School. He also became an Advanced EMT and was one of ten Americans to complete the Belgium Commando Course.

After departing the Army, Thomas served as a counselor for problematic youth. He is a national spokesperson for the Hero Fund and the Special Operations Warrior Foundation which provides college educations to the children of our special operations personnel killed in combat or training.

Keni is also a highly sought after motivational speaker and has done numerous speaking engagements for organizations ranging from Fortune 500 companies to the Boy Scouts. Thomas has made numerous appearances on every major television network including a featured story on Good Morning America and specials on The History and Discovery channels. As a country singer, his dedicated work on behalf of our veterans has been recognized by Congress and the National Defense Foundation. He is also the recipient of the American Patriot Award and The Carlton Sherwood Media Award.

He has also made numerous appearances as a military analyst on CNN Headline News, Hardball on MSNBC, Frontline on PBS, NBC Dateline, Hannity & Colmes on Fox News. The military definitely helped shape Keni into the man he is today but there is more to him than just his heroic and inspiring military background. Keni is an amazing Country Music artist and songwriter. His music appeal is reaching far beyond the boundaries of his hometown beginnings of Columbus, Georgia. This southern rocker is indeed reaching a global audience. Sharing the stage with artists like Trace Adkins, Wynonna Judd, Keith Urban and Brad Paisley just to name a few. Thomas and his band Cornbread has been touring steadily both nationwide and abroad as well as performing numerous times overseas for our troops. Keni has even went over with fellow Army veteran and Hero of the Stage alumni Craig Morgan and performed for our men and women in uniform. Keni's band Cornbread got its name actually from his nickname he got in the Army. Keni himself got the nickname because he was the only one who loved the cornbread from the MREs. The guys he served with starting calling him that and giving him their cornbread.

A very impressive list of guest artists came forward to lend their voices on Thomas' debut album, "Flags of Our Fathers: A Soldier's Story." Recorded as a tribute to our troops and their families, the disc is a stellar collection of songs written or co-written by Thomas that tell the stories inspired by life in the military and by those who serve our nation. The album was produced by the five-time Grammy award winning producer, Brent Maher, and noted songwriter, Mark Selby.

Special guest artists on the album include Vince Gill and Emmy Lou Harris, Michael McDonald, the unmistakable voice of Kenny Rogers and more…

When Keni made his debut performance on the stage of Nashville's famed Grand Ole Opry with, his song "Not Me" The performance, which received a standing ovation, was also simulcast to Iraq for his brothers and sisters in the military on Armed Forces Television in connection with the Army's outreach program, "America Supports You." Thomas, also as an ambassador for "America Supports You" performed a Salute to Our Military Men and Women concert at the Pentagon Courtyard in D.C. The event was hosted by then Secretary of Defense Donald H. Rumsfeld and was broadcast on Armed Forces Television to 170 countries worldwide.

He and his band have traveled for years to the Middle East, volunteering their time as part of the USO's "Hope and Freedom" holiday show. Keni and Cornbread even made the jump to Hollywood as the featured band in the Disney/Touchstone blockbuster, "Sweet Home Alabama."Keni was also a consultant for the movie based on himself and fellow Task Force members "Black Hawk Down" and also a consultant on the Mel Gibson movie "We Were Soldiers."

Keni has also performed the National Anthem for the New York Yankees several times, including game 1 of the 2009 World Series as well as for the San Francisco Giants on Memorial Day in 2010.

Keni has traded in his rifle for his guitar and today he is using country music as a platform to share his story of service, survival and salvation. Keni said, "When I handed in my rifle, this was my passion (music). This is what feeds my soul. Use the gifts you have been given." Thomas also says, "Do what feeds your spirit and the people around you will be better for it. I promise you they will."

A large portion of his album sales goes to the military organizations he supports. Keni also spends most of his tour dates and the holidays performing for our troops. Keni is a national spokesperson for the Hero Fund and the Special Operations Warrior Foundation which provides college educations to the children of our special operations personnel killed in combat or training.

"I know what those folks go through and I know what it means to them. Going playing for 100 guys at a forward operating base high in the mountains of Afghanistan with just my guitar is the most gratifying set I will ever do, until the day that I die. I know what those folks go through. They are being asked to do something that we take---we take it for granted." Keni Thomas is a real American Hero and has never forgotten where he comes from and he loves his brothers and sisters in the Armed Forces and gives back every chance he gets and he is a Hero of the Stage...

Country music singer Keni Thomas entertains United States Forces-Iraq service members Dec. 18. Thomas, a former Army Ranger, visited FOB Union III with the Sergeant Major of the Army Hope and Freedom Tour 2010, a USO-affiliated holiday tour throughout Iraq. *Photo by Sgt. Eunice Alicea Valentin*

Country music star Keni Thomas plays the piano just before meeting troops at Camp Arifjan, Kuwait, Dec. 12, 2007. A host of stars and entertainers are traveling as a part of the Sgt. Maj. of the Army's Hope and Freedom tour to entertain deployed troops. *Photo by: Spc. Christopher Grammer*

Country Musician, Keni Thomas, a former U.S. Army Ranger and recipient of the Bronze Star Medal for Valor performed for more than 5,000 service members at the Sergeant Major of the Army's Hope & Freedom USO Tour Dec 14. Vince Morris and Sheryl Underwood were just two of the entertainers who performed. *(Photo/Maj. Michele R. Sutak, Third Army/U.S. Army Central Public Affairs Office)*

Keni Thomas (Far Left) back during his time in the United States Army *(Keni Thomas Collection)*

HERO OF THE STAGE

Photo by Spc. Jones

Keni Thomas (U.S. Army)

"Courage is not the absence of fear but rather the judgment that something is more important than fear."

author unknown

ROCKIE LYNNE

(United States Army)

Rockie Lynn Rash was adopted in to a North Carolina family in 1964. His love of music began at an early age when he bought a used guitar from a family member and mimicked Jimmy Hendrix and Kiss on the records he listened to. He began writing and singing his own songs when he was just 14 years old. He also had to hide in the closet when he did so, because his family was very firm in their Baptist roots. He played in the jazz band at school and then joined local rock bands in his pursuit of a musical career.

After graduation, Lynne joined the US Army, where he signed up with the 82nd Airborne Division. After three years serving the military, he took advantage of the GI program and went to the Guitar Institute of Technology in Los Angeles. After completion of the program, he moved to South Carolina where he met a man named Mike Shane, who was also a musician. Together, they made the move to Nashville in the early part of the 1990s.

Lynne started out working for Noel Haggard, who is Merle Haggard's son, and The McCarter Sisters as a back-up musician. While he worked and rehearsed with them by day, he wrote his own music at night. After some hard luck, he ran in to a music insider who sent him on to Universal South Records in 2005.

Once he signed with the agency, he dropped his last name and began singing under the Rockie Lynne moniker. He recorded an album in 2006 which produced a hit called "Lipstick". It spent an impressive 10 consecutive weeks in the # 1 slot on Billboard's Country Single Sales Chart. The album didn't generate any other big hits and he parted ways with them in 2007. In 2008, he had a single called "I Can't Believe It's Me" released through the Robbins Nashville record label. The song hit the Hot 100 billboard chart, but failed to crack the Top 40. Lynne is definitely a musical success with his talent. He has appeared on the Grand Ole Opry stage 14 times and made countless media appearances. He is a popular stage performer and often goes overseas to perform for the troops. He recently launched a 21 day concert event that toured all of the US military establishments in foreign and war torn countries.

In 2010, Lynne released an album called Songs For Soldiers. All proceeds for this event are going to various charity organizations that benefit the troops. The inspiration for the album came from his 21 day tour of Afghanistan and Southwest Asia, and the Persian Gulf where he and his band performed for the troops. He also performs annually at the

Walter Reed Medical Center on Memorial Day. Rockie is also the co-founder of an annual charity motorcycle ride called TRIBUTE TO THE TROOPS, where riders visit the homes of the families of our fallen soldiers to acknowledge them for having made such a noble sacrifice. This organization has raised over $200,000.00 in aid to the families of the fallen. Rockie, like all the performers in this book, have actually raised their right hand and sworn to protect and preserve the Constitution of the United States of America and he knows what it means to have served in uniform. Rockie continually brings great credit upon himself, this nation and to the men and women of the Armed Forces and he is a Hero of the Stage...

Country music singer Rockie Lynne rides among the 50 wounded troops and 200 supporters that took part in the two-day, 110-mile Face of America Bike Ride from Gettysburg, Pa., to the National Naval Medical Center in Bethesda, Md. Lynne rode the first day's 55 miles to Frederick, Md., where the riders spent the night. Defense Dept. *Photo by Linda D. Kozaryn*

Country music singer, songwriter and lead guitarist Rockie Lynne speaks with wounded service-members during a visit to the Pentagon May 12, 2006. *Photo by Susan Levy, courtesy of Universal Records*

HERO OF THE STAGE

Defense Dept. photo by Helene C. Stikkel

Rockie Lynne (U.S. Army)

*"The Soldier above all other people,
prays for peace, for he must suffer and bear
the deepest wounds and scars of war."*

Gen. Douglas MacArthur

SONNY JAMES

(United States Army)

The 40th Annual CMA Awards (ABC), November 6, 2006
Shown from left: Sonny James and wife Doris. *(ABC/Photofest)*

SONNY JAMES LODEN was born May 1, 1929 in Alabama. He lived with his family on a small farm, where they had few crops and animals. His parents were also musicians, which is where he developed his love and talent for the music. Saturdays were spent in the home, with friends and family members coming over to sing and play their instruments. His sister Thelma was a talented singer, musician and also a comedian, even at her age of 8 when they began formally singing as a group. James was just three years old at the time, but he managed to keep pace with the group. His family was so talented, that they earned a regular spot on a local radio station playing music on Saturday nights as the Loden Family. They also won contests and got to travel around the region, playing at school auditoriums and at outdoor fairs and for other radio stations.

In three short years, the family was very popular in the region. They sang a variety of hit songs at the time and were invited to be the opening act for other touring acts coming through the region. They were in high demand and had a full schedule during the years on the road. The family band continued touring and singing until the late 1940s. Then his sister and the other child they raised that sang vocals got married and left the group in 1949. James' mother and father were content to stay closer to home and sing for the local radio station and buy a clothing store.

During this downtime in the family band, James finished his high school education and signed up with the Army National Guard in 1950. He worked in the family clothing business his mom and dad opened up and played and sang with his own band at night. It was only a few months later that the Korean Conflict was building and he was needed to help his country.

James left his home and went with the 252nd Truck Company to train at Fort Lawton in Seattle. James continued to tinker with his music and entertained his fellow troops with second hand instruments while they trained. James and his fellow troops were shipped to Korea were they completed several support missions successfully. He even wrote several songs in his down time. James left Korea and returned home in 1952 with several pages of original songs.

James only stayed in Alabama for a few weeks after his return before he packed his bags and headed to make a career in Nashville. One of James' roommates had been Chet Atkins, who had already been a player in Nashville. Atkins introduced James to meet Ken Nelson, who was the producer for Capitol Records. The record label asked him to drop his last name, which is how he came about as being the act 'Sonny James'. For several years, James worked on recordings for the record label, sang on the radio and toured with other acts. While James worked on his recordings, he met Slim Whitman and became his opening act. Whitman and James were moral men who never smoked or drank. Due to his morals, James never played in the honky tonks or bars like most other country stars did.

In 1956, James got his big release with the song called, "Young Love". He met and married his wife Doris in 1957. This was a busy time in James' career as he became a regular face on the show The Ozark Jubilee. He was also a regular on such popular shows like Ed Sullivan and Bob Hope. Those two shows gave him a large audience to find his music in both the country and the pop markets.

James focused on Nashville and in 1962 he became a member of the Grand Ole Opry. Due to his popularity with the live crowds, he decided to pick up his guitar and record new music to please the fans. This began his streak of #1 songs that lasted through five years. Each of 16 consecutive songs went to the #1 position.

In 1967, James got to be the host of the very first CMA Award Show. He was honored as being named the artist of the decade for the 1960s. He continued to record music and play concert halls during the 1970s. Between 1960 and 1979, James spent 57 weeks in the #1 position on the billboard charts.

During James' thirty year career, which ended in 1983,

he produced 72 hit songs. He decided to stop actively touring and recording music and focus on being a husband and friend to those around him.

In 1971, he received a star on the Hollywood Walk of Fame for his role on various TV shows. In 1987, he was inducted in to the Alabama Music Hall of Fame. James was inducted in to the Country Music Hall of Fame in 2006. James and Doris still live in Tennessee where they are active in many charitable organizations. The day it was announced he would be inducted into the Country Music Hall of Fame, Kix Brooks (Brooks & Dunn) said, "This is an artist who really dominated his time in history." Mr. Sonny James is known as "The Southern Gentleman" and that he is and so much more. He answered the call of duty during the Korean War and has always been a man of the utmost integrity and grace and he is a Hero of the Stage...

"Live for something rather than die for nothing."

Gen. George Patton

HERO OF THE STAGE

Sonny James (U.S. Army)

The 40th Annual CMA Awards (ABC), November 6, 2006
Shown from left: Kris Kristofferson, Sonny James *(ABC/Photofest)*

"All it takes for evil to succeed is for good men to do nothing."

Edmond Burke

RYAN WEAVER

(Ryan Weaver Collection)

(United States Army)

RYAN WEAVER... A high energy, all-American, rockin' country music artist who proudly serves as an active duty soldier, Chief Warrant Officer 3, in the United States Army. To understand Ryan Weaver and his passion for music, you need to hear his unique story: Ryan Weaver's life is an example of how an individual's dedication, discipline, focus and perseverance can help them to achieve greatness in the face of adversity.

Ryan was adopted at 10 months of age, along with his older brother Aaron, by the Weaver family. Ryan grew up living all over the state of Florida, one of eight siblings, and the youngest of three Weaver boys. Older brothers Steve and Aaron joined the military and attended flight school. When his time came, Ryan followed in their shoes. Three Weaver boys. Three Army Warrant Officers. Three helicopter pilots.

Ryan's brother Aaron died in 2004 when the Black Hawk he was a passenger in was shot down by enemy fire in Iraq. At that time, Ryan was also deployed in Iraq as a Black Hawk helicopter pilot. Ryan certainly understood mortality and the risks of combat, after all, Aaron had survived the bloody 1993 battle in Mogadishu, Somalia that became the basis for the movie, Black Hawk Down. When Aaron died, however, something changed for Ryan Weaver. He returned from combat and took a position training the next generation of Army aviators and officers at Fort Rucker, Alabama, and has not piloted a Black Hawk since that fateful day.

In July 2004, six months after the death of his brother, Ryan attended a Jeffrey Steele concert at a local Alabama club. During Steele's show he performed a song titled "Nineteen," about a boy who joins the military and dies in combat at the age of nineteen. The song touched Ryan and he shared his personal story with Steele when he met him in the autograph line after the show. In 2007, Ryan began traveling to Nashville on a regular basis to write and record his music. It was on one of those trips to Music City that Ryan re-connected with Steele. "I got a meeting with Jeffrey Steele," explains Weaver. "He recalled meeting me at that concert in Alabama [in 2004] and remembered my story." As fate would have it, Steele not only remembered Ryan Weaver, but agreed to produce him. The first song they recorded together was "Nineteen."

Currently stationed at Fort Rucker, Ryan spends his weekends and free time writing and recording music, as well as performing at fairs, festivals and clubs in the Southeastern United States. He is actively involved in charity work with the American Cancer Society and various military supporting organizations, and has performed on numerous television shows and at various events in support of those causes.

Travis McVey Interview with Ryan Weaver

Q1: What branch of service did you serve in?
A: *"United States Army"*

Q2: When and why did you join the Army?
A: *"July 23 1991, I joined to follow in my two brothers' footsteps and to serve my country."*

Q3: What unit were you with while in service?
A: *"I've served with several units: World Class OPFOR, Battle Command Training Program Ft Leavenworth, KS twice; 1st BDE, 5/14 Inf Bn then 2-5 Inf Bn/ 25th Infantry Division; Lawrence Recruiting Station/ Kansas City Recruiting Battalion; B Co 2-501 Avn RGT/4th AVN BDE of the 1st Armor Division as a Blackhawk Aviator, then the Warrant Officer Career College."*

Q4: What was your military job (MOS)?
A: *"I enlisted and spent 9 years as a Military Intelligence Analyst before attending flight school in 2000, where I became a Blackhawk Aviator."*

Q5: Where were you stationed when you were in the service?
A: *"I went to basic training at Ft Dix, NJ, Military Intelligence School at Ft Huachuca, AZ, then was stationed at Ft Leavenworth, KS and Schofield Barracks, HI before attending flight school at Ft Rucker, AL. As an Aviator, I have been stationed in Hanau, Germany and Ft Rucker, AL."*

Q6: What is the single biggest lesson you have learned in the service?

A: *"I've learned that my character, above all else, is my greatest asset. I've learned that people view military service members with a respect that is humbling and given with open trust. I would never take that trust for granted by tarnishing my character."*

Q7: Why did you decide to get out of the military?

A: *"I'll retire with 20 years, 7 months and 8 days when I'm officially done on March 1ˢᵗ 2012. It's time to move on to a new phase in my life. It's time to start chasing my dream of music full time."*

Q8: In your view, how has the military changed, if at all, since you were in?

A: *"The military is almost a completely different animal since I enlisted. Many people would say it's worse; many would say its better. I would say one thing, and that is especially since Sept 11ᵗʰ, 2001, we have become a military supported by a great country. That hasn't always been the case. I feel fortunate to have served when Americans have all stood united behind us; regardless of whether they supported the conflicts we were fighting. September 11ᵗʰ changed this country, and I was able to see that from a unique perspective. The true American love of country is not about politics when it comes to supporting our Nation's sons and daughters."*

Q9: What is your favorite memory from your military service?

A: *"The day my brothers Steve and Aaron, both Warrant Officers as well, pinned my wings on when I graduated top of my class in flight school. That was one of the last times we were ever together. The accomplishment was great, but having them there was priceless."*

Q10: Any funny or interesting stories from when you served?

A: *"With so many duty stations, training deployments and being deployed to Iraq, I have more funny and interesting stories than I could put here. Those would take a book on their own. There is one I can relate to music… On a USO tour visit from Darryl Worley and Mark Wills when I was deployed, I told Mark Wills I wrote a song that I thought was pretty good. I also said I hoped to see him at the CMA's the next year. He chuckled when I said it. Yeah, that was in 2003. I went to the CMA's for the first time last year and was there as an audience member. I found out when I really started chasing my dream to be an artist in country music that things can move slowly, and I'm sure that's why he laughed when I said it."*

Q11: What did you take away from the service that has helped you enjoy your current success?

A: *"I'm sure everyone that knows me would undoubtedly say the discipline and drive I have gained from the Army could be two of the strongest character traits they know about me. When I started pursuing my music career and learning more about the business side of it, I found quickly there are many reasons to pack it up and go home if you don't have either of those. I've heard so many stories about success with the great artists in the industry. The two things that remain consistent through most of those stories is their unwavering drive and the discipline required to continue on the path of success. I would only hope that I can follow in their footsteps."*

Q12: What impact and influence did your service have on your music?

A: *"The best thing about country music is the stories you find in amazing songs that you remember for a lifetime. I don't ever want people to forget the sacrifices of military personnel like my brother Aaron, and I think that my music finds a balance between celebrating life and bringing awareness to more serious issues like pride in our military service members. I have always loved to sing and even write, but I don't think I would have the passion and discipline to pursue music as a career had I not served. I have a wide range to the types of songs I love to perform. From more serious songs to rockin', kick butt country, I like to find a balance that doesn't overpower one with the other. After all, I have serious stories to tell, but I love to have a great time just the same."*

Q13: How do you think music affects the morale of the troops?
A: *"Without question- immeasurably. I have several friends that have spent more time away from their families in the past ten years than they have with them. Music connects you to the things that you love the most. One of the things I like to say is that I love making people forget about the hardships in their lives three minutes at a time. I know that music was comforting and motivating when I was deployed. It made me think of everything that I hold dear. No matter the situation, if I put my headphones on, the music would take me where I wanted to go. It's a beautiful thing."*

Q14: How can artists today use their military backgrounds to help today's Veterans?
A: *"To those serving or who have served, there is a very real connection with artists that have served in the military. I had the chance to open for Darryl Worley and Craig Morgan, and meeting*

them meant a great deal to me because of their previous military service. Music is the perfect way to send a message of support and understanding, and though all of country music is amazing when it comes to military support, it really does make a difference when the artist has been there and you feel they can relate. It's not just the song the artist sings, it's who they are that country music listeners want to get to know. In today's culture, having a real and tangible experience with the artist is more needed than ever."

Q15: What advice would you pass on to today's youth?
A: "I come from a small town and a big family of step, half and real siblings. I come from a family that moved around many times, saw many different life changes and faced a lot of hardships. I use those experiences to motivate me because I choose to. A message I always send to the younger audiences is that we have the freedom in this great country of ours to choose our way of life. They need to know that they can achieve anything if they put their heart and mind to it. No matter the difficulty, there is a way around it, over it or through it. I choose to call road blocks speed bumps instead. I encourage them to do the same and sometimes they may be slowed down a little, but to keep moving forward to accomplish their goals. "What remains if you dare not dream?" is one of my favorite questions to ask them."

Q16: What is your favorite charity?
A: "Can't narrow that to one. The American Cancer Society and any military supporting charities. Hard to narrow it down when they are helping my brothers and sisters. So many great causes, so little time."

Q17: Who is your favorite country music artist of all time?
A: "Jeffrey Steele. Though he's known more for his amazing writing, anyone who has never seen him perform as an artist has truly missed out on one of the best experiences in country music."

Q18: What is your favorite war/military movie?
A: "Blackhawk Down- Aaron fought in and survived the actual event that this movie portrayed. I can't help but watch that movie and think of how much Aaron was a hero and we didn't know it until this came out. I watched this movie the first time and realized just how much he went through and how fortunate I was to have him come home."

Q19: What is your favorite song?
A: "It never stays the same, honestly. I love so many different songs for so many different reasons. The last song I played on my IPhone was "Bet Yo Mamma" by Chuck Cannon. I love that song."

Q20: Who is your favorite military leader of all time?
A: "My brother Steve, who retired as a Chief Warrant Officer 4, Kiowa Aviator. I could have picked a lot of people with high rank and many accomplishments, but he's the second greatest man in my life other than my father for many reasons, to include his leadership influence in my military career and personal life. There isn't a single person I know that doesn't have the utmost respect and admiration for his leadership qualities. When he speaks, everyone really wants to hear what he has to say, because they know it will have an impact. I always use a quote to describe the kind of leader he is and I hope to emulate. "Good leaders influence people to do or

become something. Great leaders inspire those around them to do or become something special." That's my brother."

Q21: Who is your Hero?

A: "Aaron Weaver, my brother, who sacrificed his life for this beautiful country of ours. He had a choice to stay home, but he couldn't let his brothers and sisters in arms fight for what he cherished with all of his heart; for his family's ability to live free in a nation where all dreams are possible. He saw death, destruction, chaos and hate in his life, and through love he chose to face danger yet again, knowing fully he might lose his life protecting us from having to see it ourselves. There is no better definition of "Hero" in my eyes."

Ryan is one of those people you meet and just know that he is one of the good guys. He comes from a family that understands the meaning of service and sacrifice. He proudly has served his Nation and truly understands the words "Some gave some and some gave all." Ryan Weaver is a Hero of the Stage…

Brothers and Army Helicopter Pilots Aaron and Ryan Weaver in Iraq. *(Ryan Weaver Collection)*

L-R: Aaron Weaver, Ryan Weaver, Mike Weaver (Father/USMC), and Steve Weaver. This photo was taken at Flight School graduation day for Ryan where he graduated at the top of his class. This was the last picture taken of all the brothers together. Three Weavers, three Army Warrant Officers, three Helicopter Pilots. *(Ryan Weaver Collection)*

HERO OF THE STAGE

(Ryan Weaver Collection)

Ryan Weaver (U.S. Army)

"We few, we happy few, we band of brothers;
For he today that sheds his blood with me
Shall be my brother."

Shakespeare – "Henry V"

TOM T. HALL

(United States Army)

TOM T. HALL was born May 25, 1936 in Olive Hill, Kentucky. His father had purchased a guitar for Hall when he was only eight years old and since he had already begun to write poetry, learning to play it and write songs was a natural progression. His family encouraged his musical talent, but that was until tragedy struck. Unfortunately, his mother died when he was just 11 years old and it affected him and his father in a profound way. He still played his guitar and wrote music, but when he was 15 years old he had to drop out of school and get a job to support himself and his dad, who had been shot in a hunting accident and could no longer work.

The job Hall took was within a garment factory, where he met other interested people and they formed a band. This band was called the Kentucky Travelers. The band played locals gigs at the radio station and at clubs. They also played before movies started in theater houses. Hall split from the band and decided to become a DJ for the radio station the band played for in Morehead, Kentucky.

Hall decided to leave the radio business and he joined the United States Army in 1957. After training, he was sent overseas to a base in Germany. Hall wrote songs and performed them for his fellow troops in their down time. He was also a regular on the Armed Forces Radio Network, which gained him some recognition.

In 1961, Hall left the military and enrolled in Roanoke College as a journalism student. Hall also began working as a DJ for a radio station in Salem, Virginia as a way to support himself. It was at this job that his career as a songwriter and musician began. A man by the name of Jimmy Key was in the area and stopped to visit the radio station. After listening to a few of the original songs Hall wrote, he offered him a contract as a songwriter for his label, New Key Publishing.

The first of Hall's songs to be a hit on the radio was one called "DJ For a Day" in 1963. A second song called "Mad" was a hit in 1964 and convinced Hall that he needed to move to Nashville and pursue a career full time. Since Hall's songs were doing well, he was pressured in to signing a contract with Mercury Records to perform his own songs. In 1967, he had a hit with "I Washed My Face in the Morning Dew". Two more songs were released but did not have a following or make the Top 40 chart.

The next year, Hall had renewed success with a song he wrote called "Harper Valley PTA". "Harper Valley PTA" was sung by Jeannie C. Riley and it was named Single of the Year at the CMA Awards in 1968. It was also nominated for and won a Grammy Award. Once people saw he wrote the song, his music began to sell again. He had his first Top 10 hit with a song called "Ballad of Forty Dollars".

Hall kept writing songs and various artists took them to the charts during the late 1960s and in to the early 1970s. The artists that sang his songs included Loretta Lynn, George Jones, Bobby Bare, Johnny Cash and Waylon Jennings. Hall became a regular on the show Hee Haw, where he also sang and performed in the comedy skits.

During his career, Hall wrote eleven #1 songs. He was inducted in to the Country Music Hall of Fame in 2008. He has also authored nine books which cover songwriting, an autobiography and some humor collections.

Hall said he was officially retiring in 1986. In 1996, he released an album called "Songs From Sopchoppy." Alan Jackson also released a Hall song called "Little Bitty" from that album which went to the #1 spot in 1996. Hall still writes music for the country and bluegrass genre. He has a studio in his house where he and his wife allow musicians to come in and use occasionally. Mr. Hall is a Country Music Icon and served our great Nation in and out of uniform with his many talents and he is a Hero of the Stage...

HERO OF THE STAGE

Tom T. Hall (U.S. Army)

Johnny Cash Christmas (December 6, 1979)
shown: Anne Murray, Johnny Cash, Andy Kaufman,
June Carter Cash, Tom T. Hall. *(ABC/Photofest)*

PART THREE

UNITED STATES
AIR FORCE

Willie Nelson

Mel Tillis

"For once you have tasted flight you will walk the earth with your eyes turned skywards, for there you have been and there you will long to return."

Leonardo da Vinci

WILLIE NELSON

(United States Air Force)

WILLIE NELSON was born April 30, 1933 in Abbott, Texas. His family was very musical and encouraged his talent as a child. Nelson first learned how to play music when his grandparents purchased mail order lessons and gave them to him at age six. It was by age seven when he had composed his very first song. Nelson had already joined a band by the time he was nine years old.

Nelson's family owned a farm and his job was to pick cotton. Since he hated doing it so much, he decided to earn money in other ways. That included singing in local taverns for tips. In high school, Nelson toured with a band called the Bohemian Fiddlers, where his brother in law was a member.

Nelson graduated from high school in 1950. During this time, the Korean War had broken out and he decided to join the United States Air Force. He was stationed at Lackland Air Force base in San Antonio, Texas. Willie had to leave the Air Force shortly afterward (9 months) because he became plagued by back problems and was diagnosed by a doctor with this problem. Once he was released from the military, he attended Baylor University for two years studying agriculture. While he attended classes during the day, he was a DJ at night. On the weekends, he sang at clubs and honky tonks where he got lots of recognition for his talent. He quit school to focus solely on his music career that was taking off.

After he quit school, he continued to sing and write songs. In 1960, he was offered a contract with Pamper Music. He also joined Marine Corps Veteran Ray Price's band the same year. Nelson wrote "Crazy" for Patsy Cline, "Pretty Paper" for Roy Orbison and "Hello Walls" for Faron Young during his time as a bassist for Price's band.

His first album was titled "And Then I Wrote" which was released in 1962. It was such a hit, RCA Records signed Nelson to their label in 1965. He was also invited to perform at the Grand Ole Opry.

Nelson was working on a new album for RCA in 1969, but Atlantic Records wanted to secure a new deal with him. Once the deal was negotiated, Nelson became the first country artist to sign with Atlantic Records. He began a new sound called Outlaw Country. In 1973, his album titled "Shotgun Willie" was released. It did not sell well, even though music critics liked the sound. Nelson released a few more albums before switching labels again. During the 1970s Nelson began the first of many collaborations with Waylon Jennings. They released an album called "Wanted! The Outlaws" in 1976, along with Jessi Colter and Tompall Glaser.

The 1980s had several hit songs for Nelson and included

"Pancho & Lefty", "On the Road Again" and "To All the Girls I've Loved Before". In 1985, Nelson teamed up with Army Veteran Kris Kristofferson, Waylon Jennings and Air Force Veteran Johnny Cash in the Highwaymen. Their album The Lost Highwaymen was a hit.

Nelson followed his friend Kris Kristofferson in to acting in the 1980s as well. He has had roles in several movies, but did not win awards for them. Some of his movies include The Electric Horsemen, Honeysuckle Rose, Surfer Dude and The Unforeseen. All in all, Nelson has appeared in over 100 movies.

Nelson is an activist and has worked hard on many projects to better our country. One of his most important contributions has been the creation of Farm Aid, which started in 1985. Many of his friends signed on to perform during this multi-day music festival. The proceeds raised were used to help small family farmers in the Midwest from losing their farms. The festival was an annual event and is still held on a smaller scale today and has raised millions of dollars in much needed aid.

In 1990, the IRS and Nelson began a long and tenuous battle. They claimed he owed $32 million dollars in back taxes. Upon further investigation, Nelson's managers did not pay the government and they squandered away a lot of his earnings. It took until 1993 to settle all of the cases and debt.

During the 1990s and in to the 2000s, Nelson has had success with duets and collaborations with many artists. He went to #1 with Toby Keith singing "Beer For My Horses" in 2003. It won Best Video in 2004 from the ACM Awards. He and Lee Ann Womack had a hit duet with "Mendocino County Line". An album by the title "Outlaws & Angels" was released in 2004. It had duets and collaborations on it with artists such as Kid Rock, Rickie Lee Jones, Keith Richards, Joe Walsh, Merle Haggard, Al Green, Lee Ann Womack and Lucinda Williams. In 2008, Nelson worked with Snoop Dogg and created "My Medicine". Nelson has recorded close to 300 albums and wrote more than 2,500 songs as a solo artist and with other individuals.

During his career, Nelson has received many accolades. In 2005, 49 miles of State Highway 130 are named The Willie Nelson Highway. He belongs to the Library of Congress National Recording Registry. He is a trustee to the Dayton International Peace Museum, which is in honor of his activism for tolerance of all people. Nelson has won 9 Grammy Awards, 8 CMA Awards, 7 American Music Awards and 5 ACM Awards. He was voted in to the Country Music Hall of Fame in 1993. He was inducted in to the Songwriters Hall of Fame in 2001.

Nelson is a regular performer on the USO tour. He and other acts go overseas and perform for the troops in war torn countries and on military bases around the world.

During his life, Nelson has been married four times and has seven children. In the year 2004, Nelson and his wife became partners in an alternative fuel venture. They built two bio-diesel plants that produce fuel made from vegetable oil.

His first autobiography, which is self-titled, was released in 1988. A second autobiography called An Epic Life was released in 2008. Willie Nelson is one of the most familiar faces associated with Country Music and has contributed so much to the arts and entertainment of our great Nation. He has given so much of himself to others and brought much needed attention and change to some of the problems of our Country and continues that today. Willie has served our Nation in and out of uniform and supported and entertained our men and women who serve and is a Hero of the Stage...

Willie Nelson, circa 1965

The Highwaymen (ca. 1995) Shown (l-r): Johnny Cash, Willie Nelson, Kris Kristofferson, Waylon Jennings

Shown from left: (back row) Tompall Glaser, Kenneth Glancy, Jerry Bradley, Chet Atkins, (front row) Waylon Jennings, Jessi Colter, Willie Nelson, receiving awards for the album "Wanted: The Outlaws!", 1976

HERO OF THE STAGE

Willie Nelson (U.S. Air Force)

Willie Nelson and Jessica Simpson,
entertain the troops in Germany (2005)

"Music is a moral law. It gives soul to the universe, wings to the mind, flight to the imagination, and charm and gaiety to life and to everything."

Plato

MEL TILLIS

(United States Air Force)

LONNIE MELVIN TILLIS was born in Dover, Florida August 8, 1932. Even though he is famous for his music, he is also known for his stutter, which developed during his childhood as a complication of malaria. He learned how to play the drums, the violin and the guitar as he was growing up. At age 16, he won a talent show and developed a love of performing.

After high school, Tillis signed up with the United States Air Force where he was a baker. He was stationed in Okinawa, Japan and also sang in a group called the Westerners. This band entertained their fellow troops but also performed in the Japanese clubs surrounding the base.

Tillis remained in the military until 1955, and then he was discharged and moved to Nashville to pursue his singing career. He ended up being a writer first, as a song he wrote was performed by Army Veteran Webb Pierce and hit #3 on the charts in 1957. After more songs by Brenda Lee and Marine Corps Veteran Ray Price topped the charts, Columbia Records decided to sign him up to sing his own album.

Tillis' first Top 40 hit was called "The Violet and The Rose" and it was followed by a second called "Sawmill" in 1958. There weren't many more of his songs to climb the chart, so he put his focus back to writing music for others. In the 1960s, he split his time between writing and singing music.

In 1969, Tillis got his own Top 10 hit with "These Lonely Hands of Mine". After that success, he had several hits on the radio including "Arms of a Fool", Heart over Mind" and "Heaven Everyday".

Tillis was inducted in to the Songwriters International Hall of Fame in 1976. Some of the famous songs he wrote included "Emotions" by Brenda Lee; "Burning Memories" by Ray Price; "Thoughts of a Fool" by Army Veteran George Strait and "Ruby, Don't Take Your Love to Town" by Kenny Rogers. Throughout his career, he wrote over 1,000 songs and had more than 600 of them recorded by well-known artists.

Even though Tillis' songs for himself weren't as popular as those that others recorded, he still released 60 albums in country music. From those albums, 36 reached the Top 10 on the music charts.

Besides being a musician, Tillis was also an award winning actor and comedian. He was a regular singer and comedian on the Porter Wagoner Show. During the 1970s he was voted Comedian of the Year six times! Tillis appeared in popular movies, some of which included Every Which Way But Loose, Cannonball Run I and II, Smokey and the Bandit and Uphill All the Way.

In early 1981, Tillis recorded a few duets with Nancy

Sinatra, but they didn't burn up the charts. Through the rest of the 1980s, he wrote songs for up and coming stars such as Randy Travis and Ricky Skaggs. His autobiography titled Stutterin' Boy also came out during this decade. In 1993, he decided to try singing Gospel and recorded an album which did very well on the charts.

Tillis was a part of the first wave of artists to take up residency in Branson, Missouri. He built a stage and performed regular, weekly shows there from the 1980s all the way until 2002.

Throughout his career that has spanned five decades, Mel has been honored many times. In 1976, he won the CMA Entertainer of the Year Award. The Grand Ole Opry voted Tillis as a member in 2007. That was also the year he was voted in to the Country Music Hall of Fame.

Tillis also has a famous country singing daughter named Pam. She was the one who got to induct him during the ceremony at the Grand Ole Opry. Mel Tillis is a Country Music Legend and has entertained us all for many years through his music and his comedy and has served his Nation in many ways in and out of uniform and is a Hero of the Stage...

HERO OF THE STAGE

Mel Tillis (U.S. Air Force)

PART FOUR

UNITED STATES NAVY

Ronnie McDowell

Phil Stacey

James Otto

Harold Bradley

"I wish to have no connection with any ship that does not sail fast; for I intend to go in harm's way."

John Paul Jones

RONNIE McDOWELL

(United States Navy)

RONNIE MCDOWELL was born March 25, 1950 in Tennessee. Music was an important part of his life, but it didn't become integral until he was overseas. McDowell signed up for the United States Navy after high school graduation. While he was serving in the Philippines he began to sing. This solidified his love for performing.

Once he was released from active duty, McDowell focused on his music career and recorded a few songs. He worked with Scorpion Records initially, until he landed his first hit. The first song that really put McDowell on the map was his tribute to Army Veteran Elvis Presley. It was called "The King is Gone" and it was a hit on both the country and the pop charts. It has sold 5 million copies to date.

He was signed by CBS/Epic Records in 1979. With them behind him, he released a series of songs that made it in to the Top 10. Some of those songs included "Older Women", "Watchin' Girls Go By", "In a New York Minute" and "All Tied Up". "Older Women" was McDowell's first #1 song. He had eleven more songs reach the Top 10.

McDowell became friends with Army Veteran Conway Twitty as they toured together briefly. Twitty became a mentor to McDowell in the business. Curb Records signed McDowell in 1986. His first release was a duet with Twitty of the song he made in to a hit in 1958 called "It's Only Make Believe". The 1980s also saw McDowell duet with Jerry Lee Lewis. McDowell re-recorded "Unchained Melody" which became a #1 video on the country side. His talent got him to be the opening act for artists like Twitty, Loretta Lynn and Tammy Wynette. He definitely had "Old School" roots to learn from as he built his modern career. McDowell is also a part of the tribute band that plays shows that sings Elvis' songs. Since he is such a student of Elvis' work, he was asked to be the voice for the made for TV movie called Elvis and Me and Elvis Meets Nixon in the 1990s.

In 2002, McDowell recorded with Bill Pinkney and he created an album with new music that has a beach music feel to it. McDowell still tours and performs new music. Ronnie McDowell is a very talented entertainer with an amazing list of hit songs and he has a dynamic and entertaining stage presence. Ronnie has served his Nation with honor and has brought great credit upon himself and the United States Navy and he is a Hero of the Stage...

Ronnie McDowell and Lynda Lynn
a friend of my mom's at a Writers Night
performance in Nashville, TN.
(Travis McVey Collection)

HERO OF THE STAGE

(Ronnie McDowell Collection)

Ronnie McDowell (U.S. Navy)

"I can imagine no more a rewarding career. And any man who may be asked in this century what he did to make his life worthwhile, I think can respond with a great deal of pride and satisfaction: 'I served in the United States Navy."

President John F. Kennedy

PHIL STACEY

(U.S. Navy photo by Chief Petty Officer Stephen W. Hassay)

(United States Navy)

JOEL PHILIP "PHIL" STACEY was born January 21, 1978 in Harlan Country, Kentucky. He wrote his first song by the time he was six years old. Stacey grew up in Kentucky as the child of a minister, who was also the child of a minister. His family traveled between Ohio, Kansas and Kentucky throughout his early school years as they preached to congregations across the region. Stacey grew up singing in the church with his family.

Stacey, with his sister and his brother, created a group called the Stacey Trio. They performed in many contests and local venues while they grew up. Stacey gained recognition and experience as a singer and went on as a solo act, winning a state competition in Kansas.

Stacey attended Lee University in Cleveland, Tennessee where he joined a group called the Lee Singers, which was a school choir that only allowed in members through an audition. This group is very exclusive and one of the reasons why Stacey chose that college. After singing for awhile with the large group, he made it in to the smaller touring group called Second Edition. Between taking classes and singing, Stacey took a job in a recording studio so he could learn the technical aspects of being a recording artist.

Once he graduated from college, Stacey and his wife Kendra moved to Colorado where he began a career as a music minister. It was after he received a degree that the events of 9/11 happened. Stacey was so affected by the disaster that he decided to join the United States Navy to show his support for the Country and to fight terrorism. The Navy put him in a band called the Navy Band Southeast, where he became the lead singer. Stacey was first stationed in Virginia and then was moved to Florida. The group performed cover tunes to popular country acts of the time.

Stacey's fellow troops and friends encouraged him to audition for the reality show American Idol because they thought he had a lot of talent. Stacey made it to the top 5 in the America Idol competition during season 6 in 2007. He toured with the American Idol stars and also finished his four years with the Navy that summer. He is still signed up as a reservist for the Navy while working on his music career.

After he was eliminated from the show, he worked with Lyric Street Records and released an album called "Phil Stacey" in 2008. One song was released from it also in 2008 called "If You Didn't Love Me".

He signed with Reunion Records and released an album titled "Into the Light" in 2009. Reunion Records is a Christian based label. Phil Stacey is one of those men and women who when our Country was attacked raised his right hand and swore to protect and defend our Nation against all enemies both foreign and domestic and joined the United States Navy. Phil Stacey is a Hero of the Stage...

American Idol finalist Petty Officer 3rd Class Phil Stacey sings "Blaze of Glory" for approximately 850 Student Life children at Lee University during Navy Week in Chattanooga, Tenn. Navy Week Chattanooga was June 8-17. Navy weeks are designed to show Americans the investment they have made in their Navy and increase awareness in cities that do not have a significant Navy presence. *Photo by Petty Officer 1st Class Steve Owsley*

HERO OF THE STAGE

Phil Stacey (U.S. Navy)

Petty Officer 3rd Class Phil Stacey, mass communication specialist and American Idol finalist, performs live on Spokane's KHQ morning television show. Stacey's performance is part of Spokane Navy Week. Spokane Navy Week is one of 22 Navy weeks throughout the nation in regions with limited Navy presence designed to highlight the Navy's mission and thank Americans for their support. *Photo by Petty Officer 1st Class Mark O'Donald*

"The only easy day was yesterday!"

US Navy SEALS motto

JAMES OTTO

Photo Credit: David McClister

(United States Navy)

JAMES OTTO is one of the few country musicians who hails from the west coast. Otto was born July 29, 1973 into a military family in Washington on the Fort Lewis Army base and grew up all over the United States. He began his music career early and learned to play the violin and the saxophone as a child. He received a guitar for his thirteenth birthday and also learned how to play that as well. During his high school years, he spent time with his mother, who lived in Alabama, and was turned on to country music. After high school graduation, Otto joined the United States Navy and served his country.

In 1998, after he was discharged from the military, Otto decided to move to Nashville and pursue a musical career. He spent the majority of his time playing in clubs and hanging out at songwriter's nights so he could get some recognition. Otto was one of the members of Muzik Mafia, which was instrumental in launching Gretchen Wilson and Big & Rich's careers. This group held weekly shows in clubs where talent was heard and displayed for a large audience. They formed in 2001 and still play in clubs and look to launch new talent.

The Muzik Mafia also had a reality TV show which earned Otto some attention. While singing in the Nashville clubs for them, Otto met an executive with Mercury Nashville Records. They signed a deal in 2002 and worked on producing a record to release. A song called "The Ball" was released and hit #45 on the Hot 100 list and a second one called "Long Way Down" didn't make the charts at all. Since the songs weren't hits, his first album titled "Days of Our Lives" didn't get released until 2004.

Shania Twain was launching a new CD and Otto was her opening act for several shows. Another song was released from his album but failed to make the Top 40 list, so Mercury dropped him. Otto returned to working with Muzik Mafia and sang on some songs as a backup singer. During this time he wrote music and worked on singing with friends as a backup.

After Otto signed with Warner Bros. Records in 2007, he released a second album called "Sunset Man" in 2008. Otto released his song "I Just Got Started Loving You" first and it hit the #1 spot on the charts. It was also declared the #1 song of 2008 by Billboard.

In 2008, Otto co-wrote "In Color" with Marine Corps Veteran Jamey Johnson, which earned them both CMA and ACM Awards for Song of the Year. They earned a Grammy nomination but not a win for the same song.

Otto's third album is titled "Shake What God Gave Ya" and was released in 2010. He toured with Toby Keith and Trace Adkins in 2010 to generate buzz for his latest release. The first two tracks from the song did not climb the charts and he and Warner Bros. parted ways.

Otto and his wife Amy live near Nashville with their daughter. James Otto is a very talented artist and musician who is big supporter of our men and women in uniform. James comes from a long line of family service being the grandson of a Korean War Veteran, the son of a Drill Sergeant who was in the military for 23 years and being a Navy Veteran himself he is a Hero of the Stage...

HERO OF THE STAGE

James Otto (U.S. Navy)

"It seems to be a law of nature, inflexible and inexorable, that those who will not risk cannot win."

John Paul Jones

HAROLD BRADLEY

(United States Navy)

The 40th Annual CMA Awards (ABC), November 6, 2006
Shown from left: Eleanor Bradley, Harold Bradley
(ABC/Photofest)

Harold Bradley was born in Nashville January 2, 1926 to a talented musical family. (His older brother is a Country Music Hall of Fame pianist Owen Bradley). As a child, Bradley played the banjo and then learned how to play the guitar. When he was just a teenager, he played in the band for Ernest Tubb during the year 1943.

Once Bradley graduated from high school, he signed up with the United States Navy. He served for three years before he was discharged and headed to college. He took advantage of the GI Bill and studied at George Peabody College. While he studied and took classes, he also played in the bands at the Grand Ole Opry and performed with Bradley Kincaid and Eddy Arnold. This began his career as a studio musician in Nashville.

Music executives knew he had talent and allowed him in on several recording sessions with other artists. This love of recording music led him to his next venture with his brother, which was to build a recording studio in Nashville. They created Castle Recording Studios which was the first of its kind in Nashville.

This studio project lasted several years until Bradley and his brother formed Quonset Hut, which is a larger facility and could handle bigger projects. This was the start of Music Row in Nashville, which is a famous strip where all of the recording labels have offices now. This project allowed him to play accompaniment to solo artists and bands recording tracks. Bradley performed with artists Army Veteran Elvis Presley, Buddy Holly, Burl Ives, Army Veteran Charley Pride, Navy Veteran Marty Robbins and Army Veteran Conway Twitty.

Bradley's reputation as a talented and reliable musician landed him work with some of the biggest acts in the 1950s and 1960s. He worked with names such as Patsy Cline, Air Force Veteran Willie Nelson and Roy Orbison. Besides performing music, Bradley was also a well-respected producer and representation agent. He worked with stars like Slim Whitman, Eddy Arnold and Sandy Kelly as their booking agent.

Even though he worked mostly on other people's music, Columbia released three of his albums, which were all musical recordings. The first album was called Misty Guitar, the second The Bossa Nova Goes to Nashville and the third was titled Guitar For Lovers Only.

Bradley worked with his brother Owen and created 39 shows that hosted many performing acts. This variety show brought talent in to Nashville. The TV show also allowed other places in America to see what Nashville had to offer. It was a win-win situation for the musicians and TV viewers alike.

His studio also worked on recording soundtracks to various movies over the years. The soundtracks that Bradley worked on included Stay Away Joe, A Walk in the Spring Rain, Six Pack, Coal Miner's Daughter, Smokey and the Bandit II and Missing.

Bradley was an active member of the American Federation of Musicians and is a life member. Bradley served as President of the Nashville Association of Musicians Local 257 from 1991 until 2008. Bradley is a vice president to the International chapter and has served since 1999 and is still active in that role.

Despite being in his 80s, Bradley still plays his guitar. He recently collaborated with Alan Jackson's "Here In The Real World" album with Arista records. He still works with artists in recording sessions, but not as much as he used to.

Bradley has been honored many times over for his work. He was elected in the Studio Musicians Hall of Fame. He was elected to the Country Music Hall of Fame in 2006. In 2010, he was honored by the Grammy Music Association with a Trustees Award. Bradley's career has lasted fifty years and reports claim he is the most recorded guitar player in history, having worked on the most soundtracks, most songs and with the most recording artists in the studio. Harold Bradley has entertained us all for many years and still continues that tradition today. He has served our Nation faithfully in the United States Navy and has carried that tradition throughout his career of service through his music and he is a Hero of the Stage...

HERO OF THE STAGE

Harold Bradley (U.S. Navy)

The 40th Annual CMA Awards (ABC), November 6, 2006
Shown from left: Kris Kristofferson, Harold Bradley
(ABC/Photofest)

IT'S A

FAMILY TRADITION

"Families are the compass that guide us. They are the inspiration to reach great heights, and our comfort when we occasionally falter."

Brad Henry

THE PRIMARY FOCUS of this book was to highlight all of the Country Artists who have served in uniform. Not to take away from that focus but it is also important to show just a few of the many Country Artists who may have not served in uniform but proudly support and serve those that have and those that do through their many appearances. I was reminded myself recently of how caring and supportive Country Artists can be and how charitable they are. I was reminded about this a couple of times by John Rich on Celebrity Apprentice and how he defended all of Country Music and its many, many fans and showed in first class style how we step up and literally put our money where our mouths are. I believe it was the first episode where a couple of the other players made some comments about a catchy little jingle Mr. Rich had made up off the cuff literally for Camping World, an outdoor RV dealer. "Hickish country-ish" Jose Conseco had said and Richard Hatch said, "backwards." Well you could see the steam coming off that ole boy's cowboy hat when he heard that. "I will not be happy if anybody stereotypes my audience as low intelligence, or folks that can't think or have their own money," Rich said. "And if anybody in this van wants to step up on that subject I will be more than happy to square off with you about it. Please be careful when talking about my audience. Be careful about how you bring it up. Do not disrespect country music fans. To keep harmony on this team, do not challenge the intelligence of my audience." John also went on in another episode to raise $628,000.00 for the children of St. Jude Research Hospital. He raised most of that money by himself and through other Country Music artists. I know John and all the other artists feel the same way and they also feel the same way when it comes to those who would disrespect our men and women in uniform. It is well known that the one of the most supportive groups of celebrities who have given their time and volunteered to support our men and women in uniform throughout the years is country music artists. Country music partnerships with the USO started when the USO itself started. Some of the biggest names in Country Music have traveled all of the Country and been overseas many, many times performing for our troops and giving them a little taste of home and making them feel a little more appreciated. Very popular artists from the Grand Ole Opry and Gene Autry's radio show , "Melody Ranch," traveled on many USO tours, entertaining our military men and women stationed all over the world. Hank Williams, Minnie Pearl, Roy Acuff, Red Foley, Jimmy Dickens and more were among the country music artists who toured with the USO in the 1940s. This tradition continued on through the 60s, 70s, 80s, and

90s. During this time it was Johnny Cash, Patsy Cline, Roy Rogers, Dale Evans, the Judds, Lee Greenwood and more. It really is a "Family Tradition" when it comes to Country Music Artists and the Fans on how they show their respect and love for our Veterans and our men and women in uniform. That tradition continues on today with many, many artists such as Neal McCoy, Aaron Tippin, Trace Atkins, Toby Keith, Charlie Daniels and many, more visiting and performing for our service members. As a veteran myself, I can tell you first-hand how much it means when an artist comes out and visits with the troops and puts on shows to entertain them. It's kind of hard to describe unless you have been there. The closest thing I can compare it to is when you're gone from home for a long period of time and in a different country things seem to be little bit more special and sometimes it's just the small things that make the biggest impact. You can be in the jungles of Southeast Asia, the desert in Iraq or the mountains in Afghanistan and somehow or someway you get to hear a good country tune and it brings you back home for just a little while. It can bring a smile to your face on a very hard day and strike up conversations about home amongst your fellow soldiers, sailors, airmen and marines. The right song at the right time can really and does make a difference to those men and women in uniform. So, on behalf of the men and women in uniform, I would like to say thank you to all of the artists who support our troops and thank you so much for your service by traveling across this nation and going overseas to perform for them. It really, really means a lot....

John Rich, member of the country musical group, "Big and Rich," performs his song "The Man" during a Veterans Day ceremony, Nov. 11, 2008 at pier 86 in New York, home of the Intrepid Sea, Air and Space Museum. The floating museum was renovated for two years before returning to New York. Marines and Sailors from 22nd Marine Expeditionary Unit were present to celebrate Veterans Day and support the reopening of the museum. *Photo by: Cpl Brian Lewis*

Country music star Aaron Tippin poses with Marines serving in the global war on terrorism. The country music singer spent his third straight Thanksgiving entertaining service members serving in Iraq and Kuwait. 11.25.2007 *(Stars for Stripes photo)*

Legendary country star Charlie Daniels shows off his fiddle playing talents during a concert for deployed troops at Camp Liberty, Iraq, Mr. Daniels and his band finished their weeklong "Stars for Stripes" tour in Iraq. Stars for Stripes is a non-profit organization dedicated to providing quality entertainment to U.S. military forces deployed to remote locations overseas. *(U.S. Air Force photo by Master Sgt. Will Ackerman)*

Soldiers with the Regimental Fires Squadron, 278th Armored Cavalry Regiment, 13th Sustainment Command (Expeditionary) enjoy a concert performed by the Zac Brown Band. *(Courtesy Photo by: 278th Armored Calvary Regiment, Tennessee Army National Guard.)*

Task Force Ironhorse and 4th Infantry Division Deputy Commanding General - Support, Brig. Gen. James Pasquarette, presents Trace Adkins with a "Steadfast and Loyal" belt buckle as a token of appreciation to the country western music star following an autograph session at Contingency Operating Base Speicher, Nov. 1, 2010. Adkins met with troops to sign autographs and pose for photos before performing a concert as part of a United Service Organizations tour. *(U.S. Army photo by Sgt. Shawn Miller, 109th MPAD, USD-N PAO)*

Joey and Rory perform for Joint Task Force Guantanamo service members and the Naval Station Guantanamo Bay community at the Tiki Bar *Photo by Spc. Tiffany Addair*

Country music singer Billy Ray Cyrus performs for coalition forces at the USO show at Kandahar Airfield, Afghanistan. *(Photo by: Tech. Sgt. Efren Lopez)*

BAQUABAH, Iraq (May 27, 2006) -- Country singer Toby Keith (left) poses with a 4th Infantry Division Soldier during his first performance in Iraq on his current USO tour. The concert marked Keith's first appearance at Forward Operating Base Warhorse. *(Photo by Spc. Lee Elder, 133d Mobile Public Affairs Detachment)*

Master Sgt. Ricky Bakke, a logistics NCO, holds his 10-year-old daughter's guitar for country music star Carrie Underwood to sign at Camp Arifjan's Combined Operations and Intelligence Center in Kuwait. *Courtesy Photo 40th Public Affairs Detachment*

Darryl Worley performs May 2 at the Camp Victory stage, Iraq. Worley said he hoped the concert would bring a little piece of home to the Soldiers. According to his Web site, "Worley has not wavered in his support for those who put their lives on the line for democracy." *Photo by: Sgt. Samantha Beuterbaugh*

Country music singer Tim McGraw poses with a Sailor before performing a five-song musical tribute dedicated to the nation's military and their families at the Tournament Player's Club at Sawgrass during The Players military appreciation day. 5.5.2010. *Photo by: Petty Officer 2nd Class Gary Granger*

Grammy award winning musician Kid Rock, American Idol contestant and country musician Kellie Pickler and musician Zack Brown entertain troops stationed at Kandahar, Afghanistan during the 2008 USO Holiday Tour. Tour host U.S. Navy Adm. Mike Mullen, chairman of the Joint Chiefs of Staff, along with his wife Deborah, welcomed comedians John Bowman, Kathleen Madigan and Lewis Black; actress Tichina Arnold on the tour bringing music and entertainment to service members and their families stationed overseas. *(DoD photo by: Mass Communication Specialist 1st Class Chad J. McNeeley/Released)*

Country music recording artist, Chely Wright, holds up a gift received for her performance for coalition forces at Contingency Operating Base Speicher, March 2. Wright is performing throughout the Middle East as part of the Stars for Stripes tour. *(U.S. Army photo by Sgt. 1st Class Robert C Brogan)*

Country music legends Kix Brooks, left, and Bob Diprio jam out at the
Forward Operating Base Falcon Dining Facility in southern Baghdad, Jan.
28. The event was sponsored by the United Service Organizations. *Photo
by: Pfc. Nathaniel Smith*

Indiana National Guard Task Force Cyclone Soldier, Pfc. Curtis Castor, Headquarters Company, 38th Infantry Division, gets a signature from country music star Mark Wills after the USO's Sergeant Major of the Army Hope and Freedom Tour of 2009 show, at Bagram Airfield, Afghanistan. The show held world class acts like the U.S. Army's 'Downrange' Band, country music stars Mark Wills and Keni Thomas, pop rock star Alana Grace, comedian Sheryl Underwood, the dance routines of four Dallas Cowboy cheerleaders, and emcee Leeann Tweeden. *Photo by: Sgt. William Henry*

Brig. Gen. Brian Bishop, 332nd Air Expeditionary Wing commander, speaks with the members of the country music group, Lonestar, before their performance at Sustainer Theater. Bishop thanked the group for their time and support of deployed service members. *Photo by: Senior Airmen Elizabeth Rissmiller*

Big Kenny, a member of the country music duo Big and Rich, performs on the flight deck of the multipurpose amphibious assault ship USS Bataan as a way to thank the crew for their efforts during Operation Unified Response after a 7.0 magnitude earthquake caused severe damage in and around Port-au-Prince, Haiti. *Photo by Petty Officer2nd Class Kelvin Edwards*

Country music star Trace Adkins autographs a United Service Organizations' flyer for U.S. Army Sgt. Britny Roberts, 4th Infantry Division Special Troops Battalion, and a native of Carrollton, Ky., during a visit to Contingency Operating Base Speicher, Nov. 1, 2010. Adkins signed autographs and posed for photos with troops before performing a concert as part of the USO tour. *(U.S. Army photo by Sgt. Shawn Miller, 109th MPAD, USD-N PAO)*

Actor Robin Williams and rock musician Kid Rock performing for troops at contingency operating base Speicher, Iraq during the 2007 USO Christmas Tour. *Photo by Spc. Matthew Epp*

Darryl Worley (left) and his band performed at Camp Victory May 2 during their "We've Not Forgotten Tour." Worley said he hoped the tour would bring a little piece of home to the people who put their lives on the line. Since 2002, the country music star has made several visits to American troops overseas to support those who wear their country's uniform. *Photo by Sgt. Samantha Beuterbaugh*

Killeen, Texas, native, Maj. Brandon Reeves (left), brigade planner for 1st Brigade Combat Team, 1st Cavalry Division, hands a guitar to country music star Mark Chesnutt during a visit to Joint Security Station War Eagle Aug. 14. The singer signed several items for fans during the autograph session including guitars and photos. Chesnutt made several stops throughout Baghdad as part of a program designed to increase the Soldiers' morale. *Photo by Justin Carmack*

Country music artist Michael Peterson performs a song for soldiers and Department of the Army civilians assigned to United States Division-South at the USD-S Resiliency Campus stage in Basra. *Photo by Spc. James Kennedy Benjamin*

Billy Ray Cyrus, the host of NBC's "Nashville Star," performs during the open audition filming of the new season aboard the amphibious assault ship USS Iwo Jima. Footage from the event will air during the "Nashville Star" opening episode. *Photo by Petty Officer 2nd Class Gina Wollman*

Country music artist Brian Stace shakes hands and talks to U.S. service members after a concert at Kandahar Air Field. Stace says he has learned a lot about the military and the war from talking to the Soldiers on the ground. *Photo by Staff Sgt. Tony Spain*

From left: Mark Wills, Trent Willmon and Ray Scott close their, Sept. 20, 2008, show at Forward Operating Base Delta with the Eagles "Take it Easy." After the concert the singers and Valerie Waugaman, also known as "Siren" from "American Gladiators" held a meet and greet in the Morale, Welfare and Recreation center. *Photo by Spc. Allison Churchill*

Country music singer and songwriter Tracy Lawrence is greeted by Capt. Neil Parrott, commanding officer of the amphibious assault ship USS Bonhomme Richard. Lawrence visited Sailors, signed autographs and toured the ship as part of a visit arranged by the ship's Moral, Recreation and Welfare department. *Photo by Petty Officer 2nd Class Drew Williams*

American Idol contestant and country musician Kellie Pickler grants a Christmas wish for a kiss to U.S. Marine Sgt. Christopher Lambert at the 2008 USO Holiday Tour stop at Al Asad Air base, Iraq, Dec. 19. Tour host U.S. Navy Adm. Mike Mullen, chairman of the Joint Chiefs of Staff and his wife Deborah welcomed musician Zack Brown; comedians John Bowman, Kathleen Madigan and Lewis Black; actress Tichina Arnold; and Grammy award winning musician Kid Rock on the tour bringing music and entertainment to service members and their families stationed overseas. *Photo by Petty Officer 1st Class Chad McNeeley*

Country music star Toby Keith, checks out his new "Balls of the Eagle" t-shirt that was presented to him by Lt. Col. John Dunleavy, commander of 2nd Battalion, 320th Field Artillery Regiment, 1st Brigade Combat Team, 101st Airborne Division (Air Assault), at Logistical Supply Area Anaconda, Iraq, on April 28, 2008. Keith visited the 2-320th FAR to meet with Soldiers and take part in a re-enlistment at the battalion headquarters. *Photo by 1st Lt. Jonathan Springer*

Two pilots from Oklahoma serving with 1st Battalion, 111th Aviation Regiment stand with Carrie Underwood, a native of Checotah, Okla., while holding an autographed Oklahoma state flag at Camp Arifjan's Combined Operations and Intelligence Center in Kuwait. *Photo by 40th Public Affairs Detachment (Courtesy)*

Spc. Justin Lannom, of Wilson County, Tenn., receives an autograph from Aaron Tippin after Tippen's concert. Tippin, a platinum-selling country music artist, and his band played a show for the Camp Adder community at Memorial Hall. Tippin was on tour with the Star for Stripes organization, which entertains the troops overseas. Tippin takes the time every year during Thanksgiving to go overseas and perform for the troops. *Photo by Pfc. Khori Johnson*

TAPS

❖

Day is done, gone the sun,
From the hills, from the lake,
From the sky.
All is well, safely rest,

God is nigh.

ROD BRASFIELD
U.S. Army Air Corps
AUG 22 1910 † SEP 12 1958

HOMER HAYNES
U.S. Army
JUL 27 1920 † AUG 7 1971

BOB WILLS
U.S. Army
MAR 6 1905 † MAY 13 1975

ELVIS PRESLEY
U.S. Army
JAN 8 1935 † AUG 16 1977

MARTY ROBBINS
U.S. Navy
SEP 26 1925 † DEC 8 1982

BENJAMIN FRANCIS "WHITEY" FORD
U.S. Navy
MAY 12 1901 † JUN 20 1986

JETHRO BURNS
U.S. Army
MAR 10 1920 † FEB 4 1989

WEBB PIERCE
U.S. Army
AUG 8 1921 † FEB 24 1991

TENNESSEE ERNIE FORD
U.S. Army Air Corps
FEB 13 1919 † OCT 17 1991

ROGER DEAN MILLER
U.S. Army
JAN 2 1936 † OCT 25 1992

CONWAY TWITTY
U.S. Army
SEPT 1 1933 † JUN 5 1993

GENE AUTRY
U.S. Army Air Corps
SEPT 29 1907 † OCT 2 1998

LECIL TRAVIS "BOX CAR WILLIE" MARTIN
U.S. AIR FORCE
SEP 1 1931 † APR 12 1999

FLOYD TILLMAN
U.S. Army
DEC 8 1914 † AUG 22 2003

JOHNNY CASH
U.S. Air Force
FEB 26 1932 † SEP 12 2003

HANK THOMPSON
U.S. Navy
SEP 3 1925 † NOV 6 2007

JERRY REED
U.S. Army
MAR 20 1937 † SEP 1 2008

CARL SMITH
U.S. Navy
MAR 15 1927 † JAN 16 2010

FERLIN HUSKY
DEC 3 1925 † MAR 17 2011
U.S. Merchant Marines

*"A Nation which forgets its Heroes
will itself soon be forgotten."*

President Calvin Coolidge

CONTENT SOURCES

George Jones
Content:

http://thinkexist.com/quotation/my_heroes_are_the_ones_who_survived_doing_it/200179.html

http://www.georgejones.com/bio/index.php

http://en.wikipedia.org/wiki/George_Jones

http://www.cmt.com/artists/az/jones_george/artist.jhtml

http://www.gactv.com/gac/ar_az_george_jones/article/0,,GAC_26114_4709230,00.html

http://countrymusichalloffame.org/full-list-of-inductees/view/george-jones

http://thinkexist.com/quotes/johnny_cash/3.html

http://thinkexist.com/quotes/like/if-you-can-hold-your-listener-hold-their/382740/

http://thinkexist.com/quotes/george_jones/

Ray Price
Content:

http://en.wikipedia.org/wiki/Ray_Price_(musician)

http://www.cmt.com/artists/az/price_ray/bio.jhtml

http://www.starpulse.com/Music/Price,_Ray/Biography/

http://countrymusichalloffame.org/full-list-of-inductees/view/ray-price

http://oldcorps.org/USMC/quotes.html

Stephen Cochran
Content:

http://oldcorps.org/USMC/quotes.html

http://www.cmt.com/artists/az/cochran__stephen/artist.jhtml

http://www.gactv.com/gac/ar_artists_a-z/article/0,,gac_26071_5864043,00.html

http://en.wikipedia.org/wiki/Stephen_Cochran

https://www.facebook.com/StephenCochranMusic?sk=info

http://www.defense.gov/home/features/2008/0908_wwd/index_cochran.html

http://www.buyveteran.com/Press.aspx?id=20

http://www.countryweekly.com/news/country-singer-wants-you-buy-veteran

http://www.navoba.com/press.aspx?id=2a39990c-3af6-4c1d-98e7-b9d5044f040f

Jerry Foster
Content:

http://www.brainyquote.com/quotes/quotes/g/georgeorwe159448.html

http://www.myspace.com/jerryfostermusic

https://www.facebook.com/#!/jerryfos

http://www.songwritersfestival.com/lifetime_achievement_awards.htm

http://www.nashvillesongwritersfoundation.com/d-g/jerry-foster-.aspx

http://www.discogs.com/artist/Jerry+Foster

Jamey Johnson
Content:

http://225marines.org/

http://www.jameyjohnson.com/bio.aspx

http://en.wikipedia.org/wiki/Jamey_Johnson

http://www.cmt.com/artists/az/johnson_jamey/bio.jhtml

https://www.facebook.com/JameyJohnson?sk=app_4949752878

Josh Gracin
Content:

http://oldcorps.org/USMC/quotes.html

http://www.joshgracin.com/

http://www.americanidol.com/archive/contestants/season2/joshua_gracin/

http://www.cmt.com/artists/az/gracin_josh/artist.jhtml

https://www.facebook.com/JoshGracin?sk=app_178091127385

http://en.wikipedia.org/wiki/Josh_Gracin

http://www.gactv.com/gac/ar_artists_a-z/article/0,,GAC_26071_4888632,00.html

Jason Michael Carroll
Content:

https://www.facebook.com/#!/jasonmichaelcarroll

http://www.jasonmichaelcarroll.com/

http://www.myspace.com/jasonmichaelcarroll

http://en.wikipedia.org/wiki/Jason_Michael_Carroll

http://www.gactv.com/gac/ar_az_jason_michael_carroll

http://countrymusic.about.com/od/news/qt/JMC_on_GMA.htm

Kris Kristofferson
Content:

http://www.kriskristofferson.com/bio

http://en.wikipedia.org/wiki/Kris_Kristofferson

http://www.cmt.com/artists/az/kristofferson_kris/bio.jhtml

http://countrymusichalloffame.org/full-list-of-inductees/view/kris-kristofferson

http://www.imdb.com/name/nm0001434/bio

http://celebritywonder.ugo.com/html/kriskristofferson_trivia1.html

http://www.autograph-gallery.co.uk/acatalog/K52_Kris_Kristofferson.html

http://www.brainyquote.com/quotes/quotes/d/douglasmac382945.html

http://www.brainyquote.com/quotes/quotes/k/kriskristo197370.html

George Strait
Content:

http://en.wikipedia.org/wiki/George_Strait

http://www.georgestrait.com/

http://www.cmt.com/artists/az/strait_george/bio.jhtml

http://www.gactv.com/gac/ar_az_george_strait

http://countrymusichalloffame.org/full-list-of-inductees/view/george-strait

http://www.quotiki.com/quotes/3278

Charley Pride
Content:

http://countrymusichalloffame.org/full-list-of-inductees/view/charley-pride

http://www.charleypride.com/home/

http://en.wikipedia.org/wiki/Charley_Pride

http://www.cmt.com/artists/az/pride_charley/bio.jhtml

http://www.brainyquote.com/quotes/quotes/l/lorettalyn313377.html

Craig Morgan
Content:

http://www.craigmorgan.com/

http://en.wikipedia.org/wiki/Craig_Morgan_(singer)

http://www.cmt.com/artists/az/morgan_craig/bio.jhtml

http://www.gactv.com/gac/ar_az_craig_morgan

http://www.foxnews.com/entertainment/2011/02/17/craig-morgan-saves-children-from-fire/

http://quotations.about.com/cs/inspirationquotes/a/FamousMilita1.htm

John Conlee
Content:

http://www.johnconlee.com/bio.html

http://en.wikipedia.org/wiki/John_Conlee

http://www.cmt.com/artists/az/conlee_john/bio.jhtml

http://www.myspace.com/johnconlee

http://www.army.mil/-news/2010/09/02/44647-country-artist-john-conlee-says-thanks-at-warrior-and-family-support-center/

Keni Thomas
Content:

http://www.goodreads.com/quotes/show/94304

http://premierespeakers.com/keni_thomas/bio

http://www.pbs.org/wgbh/pages/frontline/shows/ambush/rangers/thomas.html

http://kenithomas.musiccitynetworks.com/index.htm?id=13848

http://www.cmt.com/artists/az/thomas__keni/bio.jhtml

http://www.imdb.com/name/nm0992805/bio

http://en.wikipedia.org/wiki/Keni_Thomas

http://www.standardnewswire.com/news/149931983.html

http://www.usa-patriotism.com/stars/kthomas.htm

https://www.facebook.com/kenithomas

http://www.writingsbyclaudia.com/favorite_quotes.html

Rockie Lynne
Content:

http://www.rockielynne.com/

http://www.cmt.com/artists/az/lynne__rockie/bio.jhtml

http://en.wikipedia.org/wiki/Rockie_Lynne

http://www.writingsbyclaudia.com/favorite_quotes.html

Sonny James
Content:

http://www.sonnyjames.com/

http://en.wikipedia.org/wiki/Sonny_James

http://www.cmt.com/artists/az/james_sonny/bio.jhtml

http://countrymusichalloffame.org/full-list-of-inductees/view/sonny-james

http://www.writingsbyclaudia.com/favorite_quotes.html

Ryan Weaver
Content:

http://www.weavercountry.com/

https://www.facebook.com/people/Ryan-Weaver/1460190141#!/ryan.weaver1

Tom T. Hall
Content:

http://www.tomthall.net/

http://en.wikipedia.org/wiki/Tom_T._Hall

http://www.cmt.com/artists/az/hall_tom_t_/bio.jhtml

http://countrymusichalloffame.org/full-list-of-inductees/view/tom-t-hall

http://www.starpulse.com/Music/Hall,_Tom_T./Biography/

https://www.facebook.com/#!/pages/Tom-T-Hall/109168560342

Willie Nelson
Content:

http://www.boardofwisdom.com/mailquote.asp?msgid=243372

http://www.willienelson.com/

http://en.wikipedia.org/wiki/Willie_Nelson

http://www.cmt.com/artists/az/nelson_willie/bio.jhtml

http://countrymusichalloffame.org/full-list-of-inductees/view/willie-nelson

http://www.biography.com/articles/Willie-Nelson-9421488

Mel Tillis
Content:

http://www.daquotes.com/topic/quotes-sayings/music-quotes/page/2

http://www.meltillis.com/

http://en.wikipedia.org/wiki/Mel_Tillis

http://www.cmt.com/artists/az/tillis_mel/bio.jhtml

http://countrymusichalloffame.org/full-list-of-inductees/view/mel-tillis

http://www.allmusic.com/artist/mel-tillis-p1839

Ronnie McDowell
Content:

http://www.ronniemcdowell.com/

http://en.wikipedia.org/wiki/Ronnie_McDowell

http://www.portlandtn.com/ronnie_mcdowell.htm

http://www.cmt.com/artists/az/mcdowell_ronnie/bio.jhtml

Phil Stacey
Content:

http://www.philstacey.com/

https://www.facebook.com/jpstacey

http://en.wikipedia.org/wiki/Phil_Stacey

http://www.cmt.com/artists/az/stacey_phil/bio.jhtml

http://www.brainyquote.com/quotes/authors/j/john_paul_jones.html

James Otto
Content:

http://www.jamesotto.net/
https://www.facebook.com/jamesotto

http://en.wikipedia.org/wiki/James_Otto

http://www.cmt.com/artists/az/otto_james/bio.jhtml

http://www.gactv.com/gac/ar_az_james_otto

http://www.allmusic.com/artist/p529056/biography

http://www.brainyquote.com/quotes/authors/j/john_paul_jones.html

Harold Bradley
Content:

http://thinkexist.com/quotes/top/occupation/country_singer/

http://en.wikipedia.org/wiki/Harold_Bradley

http://www.allmusic.com/artist/harold-bradley-p58724/biography

http://www.cmt.com/artists/az/bradley_harold/bio.jhtml

http://countrymusichalloffame.org/full-list-of-inductees/view/harold-bradley

ITS A FAMILY TRADITION
Content:

http://www.great-inspirational-quotes.com/family-quotes.html

http://www.cmt.com/news/cmt-offstage/1660308/offstage-john-rich-fights-for-fans-on-celebrity-apprentice.jhtml

http://blogs.tennessean.com/tunein/2011/03/07/john-rich-means-business-on-celebrity-apprentice/

BUY VETERAN
Content:

http://www.navoba.com/

http://www.buyveteran.com/Search.aspx

TAPS
Content:

http://countrymusichalloffame.org/full-list-of-inductees/

THANK A VETERAN • TRUST A VETERAN
BUY VETERAN
BuyVeteran.com

"Hey America, do you want to thank veterans and do you inherently trust a man or woman who has worn the uniform? Then support the 3 million American businesses owned by military veterans."

–National Veteran Business Owners Association (NaVOBA)

I REALLY HOPE YOU have enjoyed reading my book, "HEREOS OF THE STAGE/ Country Serving Country" and learning a little bit about these great Country Music Artists and how they served their Country and how they entertain their fans. As we have read about these artists, we have seen they have had their ups and their downs in the music business. Many, if not all, have overcome very big obstacles to achieve the level of success that they have had. All of them may not agree and then again all of them may, but I think the fact that they are all Veterans has helped them in this business we call Country Music. There is a reason "Why Veterans and Business Go Hand-In-Hand." Remember, the old Army recruitment campaign from the 1980s, in which the narrator insisted that soldiers in the U.S. Army "do more before 9 a.m. than most people do all day?" Well, this is really more than just an effective use of hyperbole; it's symbolic of the old-fashioned work ethic instilled through military training and service. The lessons learned and lived in military service like leadership, teamwork, competitive spirit, mission-orientation and ambition are the same attributes needed to succeed in business.

According to Census data, there are currently more than 3 million veteran-owned businesses and military veterans are twice as likely to own a business as non-veterans. In fact, one in seven veterans owns a business while only one in 14 Americans owns a business. Some of our nation's greatest entrepreneurs are military veterans and not all of them are Country Music Artists :). Fred Smith, founder and CEO of FedEx, served in the U.S. Marine Corps; Phil Knight, founder and CEO of Nike, served in the U.S. Army Reserve; and Ross Perot, founder of EDS and Perot Systems, served in the U.S. Navy; Sam Walton, founder of Wal-Mart and Sam's Club served in the U.S. Army. These men listed are only a few of the HEROES OF BUSINESS....

What is BUY VETERAN? Buy Veteran is a national campaign spearheaded by the National Veteran-Owned Business Association (NaVOBA) to bring the success and momentum of the national veteran business movement to all of America's 3 million veteran-owned businesses.

Recent nationwide polling revealed that it's not just the government and large corporations that want to Buy Veteran- the average American consumer wants to Buy Veteran too! In fact, two-thirds of respondents said they'd rather purchase from a veteran-owned business than a non-veteran owned business. I hope that goes for veteran written books verses non-veteran written books as well. Seriously, this is where the Buy Veteran campaign comes in.

Buy Veteran lets every day, Main Street, consumer-facing veteran-owned businesses like pizza shops, dry cleaners, plumbers, barbershops and sports bars in every city and small town in America capitalize on the trust and gratitude to help their businesses grow. The message is simple. "Hey America, do you want to thank veterans and do you inherently trust a man or woman who has worn the uniform? Then support the 3 million American businesses owned by military veterans."

If you're a veteran and own your own business, I encourage you to become part of NaVOBA and join the BUY VETERAN movement at www.navoba.com. If you're a consumer and want to thank veterans, then support veteran owned businesses and you can find them at www.BuyVeteran.com.

Again, thank you for purchasing and reading my book. By doing so you supported a Veteran and a Veteran Owned Business.

ABOUT THE AUTHOR

Travis L. McVey is an author, entrepreneur, U.S. Marine Corps Veteran, Army Reserve Veteran, Founder and Chief Veteran Officer at Hero Spirit, and Heroes Vodka. Mr. McVey is also the official spokesperson for the Tennessee's chapter of the National Veteran-Owned Business Association (NaVOBA) and the BUY VETERAN Campaign. Travis' most recent pursuit, *Heroes of the Stage / Country Serving Country*, is just one aspect of his ongoing mission to raise awareness and proceeds to help Veterans get the care and recognition they deserve. Travis, proud father and country music fan, currently resides near Nashville, TN.

CPSIA information can be obtained at www.ICGtesting.com
Printed in the USA
LVOW12s1226080714

393345LV00002B/5/P